BEYOND
— THE —
PULPIT

HIS EYES, HER EYES, GOD'S EYES

LAWRENCE & TAMARA NICHOLS

Unless otherwise indicated, all scripture quotations, references and definitions are from the Authorized King James Version © 1987; The New King James Version © 1982 by Thomas Nelson, Inc.; The New International Version 1973, 1978, 1984 by International Bible Society by the Zondervan Corporation; The Amplified Bible Old Testament © 1962, 1964, 1965, 1987 by the Zondervan Corporation; The Amplified New Testament © 1954, 1958, 1987 by the Lockman Foundation; The Message. Copyright © 1993, 1994, 1995, 1996, 2000, 2001, 2002.

BEYOND THE PULPIT
His Eyes, Her Eyes, God's Eyes

Lawrence and Tamara Nichols
LTN – LEADERS WHO WIN
c/o Sure Foundation Kingdom Ambassadors, Inc.
P.O. Box 14732, Newport News, VA 23608
(757) 741-8044

ISBN 978-1-949826-21-0
Copyright © 2020
All rights reserved

To contact the authors for materials or to schedule a speaking engagement or leadership seminar in your church or area, write, call, or connect:

ltnleaderswhowin@gmail.com
 https://www.facebook.com/LTNLeadersWhoWin
 https://twitter.com/leaderswhowin
 https://www.instagram.com/ltnleaderswhowin

Published by: EAGLES GLOBAL Publishing | Frisco, Texas
In conjunction with the 2019 Eagles Authors Course

Cover & interior designed by DestinedToPublish.com | (773) 783-2981

DEDICATION

To the best vision we could have hoped for
—our children and grandchildren.

To all of our partners in ministry and life
who sometimes grow weary along the way.

LAWRENCE & TAMARA NICHOLS

ACKNOWLEDGMENTS

First, and foremost, we give glory and honor to God, who, by His infinite knowledge and wisdom, saw fit to place this project in our hearts. Without His vision, we would not have had the courage or strength to see this through.

To our mothers, Elzader Nichols-Rand and Vivian Clegg. Thank you for your endless love, strength, and wisdom. You continue to be a source of light and encouragement to us both. Our love for you is beyond words.

To our children, Lawrence II, Jazmyn, Lamonte, Tia, Nala, Angel, and Miracle, and our grandchildren, Zoey, Josiah, and Jeremiah. You are our "why"!

To our Sure Foundation Kingdom Ambassadors Family. Thank you for allowing us the space to learn, lead, and love you all, and for giving us grace when we got it absolutely wrong. We love you!

PREFACE

This book is co-authored by two people who just happen to be married, and it explores leadership in ministry from two different points of view. *This is not a marriage book!* As you read, you'll look through the lenses of our individual experiences. Lawrence's view will be identified as "his eyes" and Tamara's view will be expressed as "her eyes." You'll know they are unique to our personal perspectives by the way the book is structured. It's important to note that while our views are different, we try to highlight some of the universal challenges everyone experiences and the universal principles we all can (and should) apply to overcome those challenges. We express those universal principles as "God's eyes."

If you're leading in ministry, then you're likely looking for solutions to answer the challenges you routinely face in your calling, your family, your ministry assignment, and your influence in any one of these areas at any given time. Well, here's some great news! *This is not that book!* This book will not solve your problems, per se. It will, however, provide you with insight, perspective, and wisdom as you travel the path. It will likely incite more questions than answers. It will cause you to look at the person in the mirror and address the issues that may be preventing you from reaching your full potential. It is our goal to teach others that, despite the challenges associated with leadership in ministry (and there are many), success is possible.

This is not necessarily a marriage book, but it is a book that will help you see your situation through the transparent lens of a leadership couple as they carry out their part of the Omniscient Creator's vision. It's a candid look at the realities of ministry and leadership, including its pitfalls, its ugliness, and, ultimately, its rewards through "his eyes" and "her eyes." It is two voices, unified with one sound, crying out in the wilderness as a reminder that your labor is not in vain and you are not by yourself. It is a brief respite with friends who understand your struggle, but are bold enough to tell you, "Get up! You still have work to do! Don't give up on God! Don't give up on yourself! Don't give up on your spouse! Don't give up on your children! Don't give up on your ministry! Don't give up on your business! Don't give up on your dreams! Don't give up on your destiny! Don't give up! You've got purpose, and purpose is waiting on you!"

INTRODUCTION

We are Lawrence and Tamara, taking you along a literary journey into leadership in ministry. Think of it as an art gallery tour where you will observe other artists' works in order to formulate, refine, and/or inform your experience. Now, before we begin, you will need four sets of lenses. We will provide two sets (aka his and her eyes); you'll bring your own set; and, like God did for us, He will provide you with His set (God's eyes). Here's the bottom line, right up front: your story is important and your struggle is real, but no one's view (not even your own) compares to God's greater plan and purpose. When you see it from His vantage point—you win!

Our story begins as two teenagers who met more than thirty years ago in a Detroit public high school. We came from similar backgrounds: both the eldest in our respective families, both from divorced homes, and both insecure and grasping for purpose in unhealthy ways. Out of this, we gave birth to a son and became teenage parents. Fortunately, for us and you, that's not where the story ended. Here is an important point to remember: where you begin doesn't matter; how you live, what you do, and how you end is what matters.

We are successful leaders in ministry. We have, according to today's standard, a large family. We have served in every capacity within the local church, including church planting. We have launched businesses, opened a school, and given our lives to purpose. Amid all of our successes, we have experienced significant struggles, made incredible sacrifices, and endured many hardships. We have tried our best to live our lives through God's eyes, but it hasn't been easy. In fact, it has been downright difficult. However, the lessons and principles we've learned along the way have all been worth every moment.

In this book, you'll come face-to-face with the demands and sacrifices associated with leadership in ministry (and anywhere else, for that matter), its cost, and the victory of walking in purpose in spite of the challenges. You'll come to understand that, regardless of the perspective, plans will be shattered, thinking reshaped, and life repurposed for God's perfect work. If you're ready, let's embark on this journey together.

Chapter 1

The Call and the Answer

Then I heard the voice of the Lord, saying, "Whom should I send? Who will go for Us?" Then I said, "Here am I. Send me!" —Isaiah 6:8, NLV

HIS EYES

We are the sum total of our experiences. Those experiences—be they positive or negative—make us the person we are, at any given point in our lives. And, like a flowing river, those same experiences, and those yet to come, continue to influence and reshape the person we are, and the person we become. None of us are the same as we were yesterday, nor will be tomorrow. —*B.J. Neblett*

I answered God's call to the gospel ministry in 2001, but somehow, I always knew I was called. If you're honest, you know it, too. You didn't wake up one day and say, "I think I'll be a (fill in the blank with whatever your assignment is) today!" At the core of who you are, you have always sensed you were created to do something significant.

There are those moments in time, however, when that inner calling and your answer meet. I can't help but think it's the moment when calling and answer collide to conceive God's purpose in each of us. It's the moment when the construction site for God's plan is identified. In real estate, property is purchased and can be used immediately or reserved for future use. The developer of the land knows the plans, the process, and what the potential future value of the land will be long before any structure of significance is ever built. The condition of the land and its surroundings often determine the amount of preparation needed to develop the land for its future use. I think it's worth noting that identification is not construction. Let me put it this way: while each of us has been chosen to fulfill a purpose, none of us arrive ready to walk in our purpose. It takes time and experience. I truly believe we are intricately predetermined for greatness (see Psalms 139:13–16), but we cannot forgo the process. Yes, I am fairly confident I was called, but I could have never imagined I would lead in ministry, plant a church, launch businesses, or even write a book!

One of the greatest mind-blowing revelations you and I will ever experience, I think, is the realized connection between who God says you are and *your agreement* with who God says you are! It is the transition from being "reserved for future use" to the activation of purpose and permission to build. That, however, is not always easy to see when you are being broken to be built. For nearly two decades, I underwent a series of experiences that shaped my perspective and positioned me to accept my purpose.

I mentioned earlier that land must be purchased before use, its purpose must be identified (called zoning), and then permission is granted to begin construction. The owner commits to the land purchase, determines what the land will be used for, and the land submits to the owner's plan for it. It's a fairly simple concept, right? Before anything is built, however, there is a groundbreaking ceremony. Everyone comes to celebrate the newness of the vision, but no one can really tell you how stressful and painstaking the process will be.

In retrospect, I can see when God "broke" my ground. I was the product of a divorced home, which resulted in a broken outlook toward family. I grew up in a financially challenged environment in inner-city Detroit, resulting in a broken outlook toward money (poverty mindset). My childhood was heavily weighted with responsibility, resulting in a broken outlook toward life. Every area of my physical, mental, and emotional environment was broken. Today, I stand amazed that the broken mess of my life was nothing more than God's breaking process to build and ultimately bridge me into His purpose.

The Challenges of Your Yes: From His Eyes

1. Be sent, but get whole

My wife and I were immersed in ministry without training wheels. I was excited, but excitement isn't wholeness. When the excitement wore off, the battle within began. My wife and I have served together in ministry for nearly a quarter of a century. During that time, I have personally struggled in my walk, my call, my personal and professional life, my leadership, and my relationships. I call it pre-ministry baggage. Ministry's call does not discriminate; it does not automatically eliminate the baggage of life. If anything, it magnifies it. Address it. Period! Unpack the bags! Otherwise, you will spend a significant portion of your time carrying bags full of insecurity, doubt, regret, and every other negative thought that tries to exalt itself against the knowledge of God (see 2 Corinthians 10:5). This war within will make you doubt, and even deny your call to leadership or avoid the mantle of your assignment. It will significantly impact your personal growth and the well-being of those around you. Remember: God did the breaking. He is more than able to remove, repair, and/or replace what is needed for you to move in the assignment. Don't fight the process!

LEADERSHIP NUGGET

Process without good discipleship can be hazardous!
Too often, leaders are quick to position people
without allowing God to prove and process them first.

2. Remember who He is

You can lose your identity in the "call." I know I have. The process of becoming whole, maintaining balance, and fulfilling God's assignment is huge. For years I quietly shouldered the weight of the primary breadwinner, of family, of sheep, of everything. I found myself depressed and disillusioned, and, honestly, I lost my joy. I had to learn to stop carrying the burden. The *Message* paraphrase says, "Pile your troubles on God's shoulders—he'll carry your load, he'll help you out. He'll never let good people topple into ruin" (Psalm 55:22). If God cares for you, then let *Him* care for you. It's His responsibility—not yours! Your call should never bring you to the place where you conduct "cave ministry" (see 1 Kings 19).

It's the place where you forget who you are because you have forgotten that God is the one who equips, enables, and empowers you to do the work. Don't go here; it's futile. God will remind you of who He is, reject your excuse for being there, send you to complete the work He assigned you, and make you train up someone to complete your assignment! Keep God first!

Her Eyes

Who knew agreeing with what God had already preordained would be so honorable, and yet so lonely? It would come with many promises, yet so many sacrifices. It would be so rewarding, yet with many disappointments. This is the reality of answering "yes" to your call. Nevertheless, leaders continue to answer with a "Yes!" Little did I know that saying yes meant saying yes to everything being a leader entailed. It meant yes, I will endure this trial without giving up. Yes, I will go through the test without trying to cheat my way out. Yes, I will commit to the vision at all cost.

When you align yourself in agreement with what God desires for your life, it requires your complete surrender, reliance, dependence, and trust. Are there struggles and challenges in ministry? Of course, but with every challenge, there's a lesson to be learned if you are willing to be taught.

The Challenges of Your Yes: From Her Eyes

3. Know who you are

LEADERSHIP NUGGET

Self-identity is one of the most crucial steps in life. If you don't know who you are, you will not know where you are going or how you are going to get there. When you lack purpose and vision you will lack access to your God-given power and authority.

My immediate struggle was in answering the question, What is my role in this local body? Am I the pastor's wife, first lady, lady elect, sis, co-pastor, prophetess, apostle? I knew I was called to lead and I knew my assignment, I just didn't know what hat to put on for the occasion. At our ordination, my certificate said Pastor. I was ordained as a pastor, but I didn't have the makeup or heart of a pastor. However, I wanted to fill that role because I thought that was what I had to do. I didn't know it was okay that I was different. I tried to be sympathetic to the issues and problems of the other women. I tried to have compassion, and I genuinely tried to connect. It wasn't that I didn't have compassion or that I wasn't sympathetic to every issue, problem, or concern.

I was just more focused on getting to the solution and knowing that the problem could be overcome. It wasn't that the opinions and past did not matter, but in my eyes, God's word mattered more. The end goal while continuing to walk in purpose was more important than dwelling on things that could be overcome with a word or a decision. However, I managed to fall right into that trap of bondage. Trying to function mis-mantled brings on frustration and exhaustion. I encourage every leader to seek God and discover who you truly are. What are *your* gifts and your passions? Remain authentic to the core. Remember, remain true to who you are.

Do not try to become what others want you to be.
Just be who God called you to be.

Before you were formed in your mother's womb, God knew you personally and intimately. He knew the plans for your life. However, life has a way of convincing us of the opposite of what God says. The Creator thought His creation was good, therefore everything about you, your personality, your giftings, your intellectual abilities, your intricate styles, your uniqueness, and every detail concerning you are all good. So, be good with the reality God has established and reject trying to live in a false reality that you were never designed to fit in. I tried to be what I was not. I was conflicted and constantly found myself in a position of always apologizing to someone because I was not the typical pastor's wife. I was not the "go-to," "cry on the shoulder" girlfriend. I was not the "pick up the phone and gossip" woman. I was not the "sit on the front row or in the pulpit with the big hats, suits and heels" kind of woman either. Nor was I the silent helpmeet in the ministry.

I tried to become what everyone else wanted me to be, and I failed. My heart was for connecting with a team of women with purpose and vision. And you know what? That's okay! I am a woman designed to pull up dead roots, pull down strongholds, shake off dead weight, replant, reproduce, empower, and equip. Deliverance from people-pleasing is beautiful and absolutely freeing. It begins with acceptance of who you really are and confidence in the way you were designed to wear your garment.

What We Learned:
GOD'S EYES

Reflecting on the years, it's safe to say that the price of our yes has been costly. Truthfully, it would be easy to gripe and complain and sing, "Nobody knows the trouble I've seen; nobody knows my sorrow." But the truth is more positive:

Every "yes" to God is permission to be tested and proven. Our calling (yours and ours) is only activated when we say yes. God won't force you into purpose. A yes to God simply means you are ready to undergo whatever is next. It is faith at full throttle, propelling you into a place you've never been, and knowing everything is going to be all right because God is in control.

Your "yes" is the stewardship key God uses to grant you next-level access. The same way a key has a dual purpose (to lock and unlock), so does your yes. Your yes lets God know that He can trust you with what the next level offers. It's proof you are ready to move from where you were to where God wants to take you.

Attitude is everything. Don't allow a negative attitude to negate your process. Yes from your mouth and no from your heart equals a no to God. The test is already demanding. The wrong attitude only sets us up to repeat the test. If you have a poor attitude, then make up your mind to adopt a winning one. Adjust your attitude and you will adjust your outcome.

Your "yes" is an opportunity to learn—embrace it. You can say yes and not fully comprehend the lesson it offers. Too often, we want to circumvent the process. Every yes is a teachable moment. God wants to develop you for His kingdom purposes by teaching you how to embrace, endure, and overcome for the level you're in and the level you're going to. Don't resist it.

Your "yes" makes you available. It has often been said that God opens doors that no one can shut. As true as that may be, an open door means absolutely nothing if you are unwilling to say yes to what that door offers. Granted, you won't know what's on the other side, but you'll never know if you don't show up to the door in the first place.

Remember, your challenges are nothing more than girders God

uses to build, strengthen, and reinforce the bridge He has already planned to bring you, and those you lead, over into purpose! As you review your life's story, you'll find that God has allowed a series of experiences to shape, move, and bridge you into your purpose while steadily moving you toward your destiny, too. The bridge is the connection between your identity and your purpose. You may not want to, but God is looking for someone who will go. You'll never walk fully in God's purpose for your life and roles (leader, servant, husband, wife, son, daughter, brother, sister, etc.) until you say *yes* to the One who knows the plans for your life (see Jeremiah 29:11).

God knows who he has called, He knows the cost of the call, and He needs you to agree and say yes.

REFLECTIONS
Questions for Discussion

1. Reflect on your personal experience when you were first called to ministry. What was your response?

2. What were some of the challenges you faced?

3. How did you overcome those challenges?

4. In what areas have you been tested and proven?

5. Do you believe God can trust you with more?

6. In what ways have you had to adjust your attitude throughout your journey?

7. In what areas do you need to continue learning?

8. Have you completely made your life available to be a usable vessel of God? If not, what are your hindrances?

Chapter 2

LEARN TO DIE TO SELF

A normal human being does not want the Kingdom of Heaven; he wants life on earth to continue.
—George Orwell

Mr. Orwell captured the crux of human existence in that statement—the battle of the wills! A quick survey of the times, a few moments on social media, or fifteen minutes of news media ticker-tape are compelling indicators that most of the world's population rejects the Kingdom of Heaven for personal gain, comfort, or both. Ulterior motives, hidden agendas, and secret covetous behavior are often the culprits keeping us from obtaining God's best. So, why on earth would we choose the world's offerings over Heaven? The stark truth is that the attainment of the kingdom (or anything else worth having) requires a death to will. Whose will prevails, however, depends greatly upon who is held in higher esteem. God's word, regardless of whether we choose to believe it, is always accomplished. Notice that we didn't say His "will" would be accomplished. God doesn't will for anyone to perish, but simply put, it happens. God never imposes His will upon anyone. Instead, will is about choice—we can choose to follow it or not. Here are two points to consider:

There are always consequences for our choices.

1. He can (and does) find someone else to fulfill His will.

2. God always desires to complete His will through the one whom

He's selected for the assignment. If God's will is best, then our will must die.

HIS EYES

When the will of God crosses the will of man, somebody has to die. —Addison Leitch

HIS PROCESS

I have spent the majority of my life sacrificing for others. This bedrock principle has served as the foundation of my leadership model. As the eldest child, and not unlike older children in many single-parent homes of the late '70s and early '80s, I filled the role of surrogate parent for my kid sister. I had a responsibility greater than myself. It was an automatic forfeiture of my right to "just be a kid." I was eight. I wasn't angry about it; after all, I was "Momma's big helper" and I wanted to make things easier for her.

The sting of it all, however, came when friends asked if I could come outside to play or when I couldn't participate in any after-school activities because of my responsibilities. I became adept at building walls of obscurity to hide my disappointment and discouragement. I had people depending on me. On top of that, I often heard the story of how my grandfather lost his mother when he was only five years old, and how there wasn't anything he wouldn't do for her if she were alive. Talk about pressure. I revered this man. Much of who I am today is modeled after who he was. I couldn't let them down.

Little did I know how much this would shape my views, inform my decisions, and affect my relationships for years to come. My premature maturity caused me to seek out more long-term relationships in sixth, seventh, and eighth grades, only to be rejected because I was "too serious." This did not bode well for my self-esteem, so instead of learning how to dial back my maturity, I sought out relationships with older girls who introduced me to sex, drinking, and anything else I thought I was old enough to do. My unhealthy view led to taking on destructive loads of responsibility and created an aversion to failure. I became distrusting of others because I had become highly self-reliant and prideful. I was a self-licking ice cream cone in the middle of the desert.

By the time I was a senior in high school, I had more responsibility than I knew what to do with. I quit high school sports so I could hold down two jobs. My grades suffered, but I still managed to graduate on time. I was still trying to meet the needs of my family and live my own life, too. For a brief moment, I enjoyed a glimpse of what life could be. For six whole months, I went off to college, only to have life rear its head.

Before the end of my first semester in college, I found out that my girlfriend (now wife) was pregnant and that I needed to return home to take care of my mom and sister due an emergent living situation. So, I went home and did what I had always done: I sacrificed for the benefit of everyone else. This time, though, it was different. I sank into a very dark place. I knew how to manage sacrifice, but I didn't know how to manage failure—failure to achieve my dreams, failure resulting in embarrassment, and failure to be what everyone expected me to be.

What I didn't know then, but I can see with absolute clarity now, was I was sacrificing, but I wasn't dying to self. I had learned how to suppress my true feelings for the benefit of everyone else. I learned how to please others. I hadn't learned to die to myself. When you truly die to yourself, there is no hidden remorse or regret and you don't keep score. I was full of these and I was angry. For years I had sacrificed, and this was the return. Don't be fooled—you can sacrifice and not actually lay down your life.

Another six years passed before I began my journey to healing and deliverance from fear, pride, and people. Honestly, I'm still on that journey nearly twenty-five years later. I'm no longer "tossed and driven," but every time I think I've got it beat, God gently reminds me by uprooting something else to let me know He's still working on me. To truly die, I have had to take some intentional steps.

1. Overcome fear

> While I thought that I was learning how to live,
> I have been learning how to die. —Leonardo da
> Vinci

My greatest fear has been failure. There—I said it. I've struggled with the fear of failure my entire life. I've missed prime opportunities because I was afraid to jump. I was worried about what the outcome might be. I didn't grow up in a home where risk was fostered or encouraged. I had to play it safe. I was expected to do the right thing because I was either being looked up to or looked at. There was no room for wrong. So, I learned to play it safe. Safe became comfortable and ultimately became a state of mind. To make matters worse, it seemed like every time I stepped out of the "safe" bubble there was some jacked-up consequence that followed.

In fourth grade, I took my bike out for a spin. Riding my bike was nothing new. I had been riding a bike for years (okay, in kid's time it seemed like forever). But today, I was going to do something different. I was going to get my bike up to top speed and jump the curb. I started at the opposite end of the block. I was really moving, moving faster than I had ever pedaled before. There it was. The curb was in view. I envisioned it. This was going to be epic. I imagined bragging to all my friends about it. And then it happened. My feet slipped off the pedals at the moment right before I reached the curb. I went over that curb and hit the high curb just across the street, right after a near-miss from the moving car that I cut in front of. I smacked hard into a fire hydrant, flipped my bike, and broke my arm. As I lay there in pain, the only thoughts that came to mind were one, I'm going to get in trouble for this; and two, if I had played it safe, this never would've happened.

I made a decision to push the boundaries and I got hurt. There was no one there to encourage me through my failure, but there sure was the criticism of "What were you thinking?" Of course, you're thinking, "This is what boys do, right? They fall down. They get back up. They try again." If it's physical failure, maybe. It depends on their tolerance level for pain. Men say it all the time: "No pain, no gain." But if it's emotional? Eh, not so much. When a man hurts emotionally, he often shuts everything and everyone down to process and bury it. I know—I have lots of experience, and I'm good at it. I've had lots of practice.

One of my earliest (and most painful) childhood memories happened during a visit with my dad when I was about eleven years old. I remember being really excited about spending time with him. It had been years since I'd last seen him and I just knew this was going to be special. He picked me up in Detroit and we traveled back to his apartment in Ohio. The next day, we started our road trip to Florida to visit my grandmother. It started off great. We played a couple of travel games, listened to some music, and enjoyed the scenery of 95 South. This was awesome! And then it started. As kids do on road trips, I fell asleep. When I woke up, I chided myself for sleeping. Not a big deal, right? But to me, it was. I didn't want to disappoint him.

I was looking for affirmation from my dad, whom I hadn't seen in years. I was searching for a respite from the weight of responsibility. I was longing for a moment to just be a kid. Instead, I found myself overtaken with that all-too-familiar feeling of failure—failure to respond in a manner acceptable to the one I so desperately needed validation from. For years I felt like I had failed in my relationship with my dad. That feeling eventually gave birth to depression, low self-esteem, and, ultimately, anger. I came to hate failure because it represented the void of things I desired most.

In life and ministry, I have failed miserably. As a leader, I know failure is not an if, but a when. It's going to happen. Even though I know it, I still struggle with it. Why? Not because of its inevitability. Instead, it's because leaders rarely receive soft places to land when they fail. It hurts. That's the price of leadership. It's not like Little League softball, where everyone encourages you to do better next time. Every leader doesn't receive a trophy for their efforts. No, the quips and comments are brash and harsh. They cut deep. The looks are sharp. People disconnect. Consolation is not your prize.

Instead, you can expect a barrage of criticism for what you did wrong. On its best day, it's as exhilarating as sailing across the Mediterranean in the summertime. At its worst, it's a soul-crushing experience that makes you question your existence. I have learned to cast my care upon the Lord.

Job, in the book of the same name, found himself broke, busted, and disgusted. He lost his wealth, family, and health. Losing everything, while devastating, is not necessarily the issue. The problem arises when our sacrifices to God become a product of our fears rather than affirmations of our faith. Now, if anyone had the right to have a pity party, most would agree that Job earned his moment in the spotlight. I don't, nor do I ever want to, know what that kind of loss feels like. There's a lesson all leaders can learn from it, though. When fear serves as our prime motivator, our actions are born out of religious activity and not relational trust.

As a leader in ministry, you will win, and you will lose; you will succeed, and you will fail. It's inevitable. What you do after the loss or the failure makes the difference, and if your relationship with the Father is based on His hand and not His heart, you can end up in self-proclaimed pity parties. Job curses the day he was born. What is interesting to note is that he says, "For the thing I *feared* has overtaken me, and what I dreaded has befallen me. I am not at ease or quiet; I have no rest, for trouble has come" (Job 3:25–26, BSB, italics added for emphasis). Leaders understand sacrifice, but it is usually with the caveat that the status quo remains undisturbed. We sacrifice for things we hope to keep. What would happen if we sacrificed knowing that it would cost everything? Until you remove the fear of losing everything you have, with the understanding that it's all temporary anyway, you really aren't ready to die to yourself.

LEADERSHIP NUGGET:

Failure is not a matter of if; it's a matter of when.

---

2. Overcome pride—the silent killer

> Pride must die in you, or nothing of heaven can
> live in you. — Andrew Murray

As I said before, my life has been one sacrifice after the next. It's
what is expected of ministry leaders, right? Herein lies the snare: I
started keeping score. Pride secretly crept in and made me numb
to the principle of sacrifice. Instead of remaining humble, I started
wearing it like a badge of entitlement. My attitude of pride caused
me to become critical. I began to make it more about myself
rather than other people. It made me feel as though I deserved
an audience with the Father regarding my situation more than I
needed an audience with Him to express my gratitude. My pride
made me more dependent on me and less dependent on God.

The Gospels tell of a man, a rich young ruler who by his own
standard has met the requirements of a sacrificial life before God.
On its face, it *appears* the young ruler has met the mark. He
answers the Lord's question with an emphatic thumbs-up! He says,
"I've done that from my youth." I can see the visual: His chest is
stuck out, his shoulders back, his head held high. He's thinking,
"I've got this kingdom thing in the bag." The Lord then drops the
whammy—sell it all and follow Me. Ouch! Get rid of my stuff and
give up my position, too? Pride is the silent killer that lurks in the
shadows of sacrifice. Until you're willing to die to yourself, you'll
never experience the life Christ has prepared for you.

LEADERSHIP NUGGET:

The most expensive thing you'll ever give up is your will.

---

3. Get over people!

> Care about people's approval, and you will always
> be their prisoner. —Lao Tzu

When you're a leader, your ability to connect with others is crucial. Connection capital is probably the most import currency you possess in this position. There are, however, unhealthy connections that will absolutely slow forward progress. In fact, these types of connections will crush your soul. I'm not necessarily one who thrives on the presence of people to feel alive, but I come alive when I'm around people. When I do, I want to connect with everyone in the room. Since I'm a leader, preacher, speaker, mentor, and coach, it's important to me to connect with those I have the privilege of pouring into. I'm also very empathetic to the feelings of others. I'm a connector, so this is both a great asset and my worst liability. But using people as a gauge for my performance kept me on an emotional rollercoaster. I had given people power to dictate my actions and had become a slave to their will. Before I became intentional about balance, I sought approval. Now I look for feedback, and seek approval from God.

LEADERSHIP NUGGET:

Seek feedback, not validation.

Her Eyes

Salvation is free, but the walk will cost you every-thing. —Apostle Lawrence Nichols

"He must become greater; I must become less" (John 3:30, NIV), the Bible tells us. Unfortunately, we live in a society that is "for the people and by the people." We live in a world that is a democracy and says we all have a say. However, because we're kingdom citizens, what we say must match what God says. Our language must be the language of our King in His kingdom. If you've ever had a mouth like I did, you know that speaking the language of the King can be challenging. It was even more challenging when I was so stubborn and prideful. Changing the way we speak is part of dying to self. God's will for your life must become your priority. In order to know His will, you have to know His character; in order to know His character, you have to know and study His word. Trust me, I know and understand the struggle of trying to remain silent when you feel like you have a voice that needs to be heard. I understand that feeling of walking away, believing that you should have said this and you should have said that. I was that dummy—yes, the dummy who thought I was doing what I had a right to do, and what I felt was right, but in reality, I was sowing seeds of divisiveness. Lord, forgive me for my mouth! Thank you, Holy Spirit, for teaching me to die to myself.

> I have been crucified with Christ and I no lon-
> ger live, but Christ lives in me. The life I now
> live in the body, I live by faith in the Son of
> God, who loved me and gave himself for me.
> —Galatians 2:20, NIV

Her Process

Have you ever had the experience of searching for something in the word, and suddenly the Holy Spirit leads you somewhere completely different? While searching out the scriptures one day for a rebuttal or reason I didn't have to do what was required, as we often do, I was heavily convicted by the Holy Spirit. I was part of the worship team/choir, and at that particular time, the standards of the ministry came with a long list of dos and don'ts.

Well, of course my opinionated, independent self had to challenge everything. I didn't understand submission, and I didn't care where or who the direction came from. If I didn't agree, you and everyone else were going to know I did not agree. My "two cents" was going to make the headlines. I had rights . . . I was so *wrong*! I was so ignorant of how I had allowed the spirit of rebellion and divisiveness to move through me—until, while searching to be right, I discovered I was wrong. While looking for scripture to prove my point, I was led to begin studying the lives of David and

Saul. At first I thought, okay, fine. I'm a worship leader, so this will be helpful. Boy, was I wrong. I was about to receive the most important lesson of my life and ministry.

4. Renounce rebellion

God was beginning to show me how my attitude was standing in the way. In 1 Samuel 15:3, Saul is given specific instructions for how to take out the Amalekites: "Now go, attack the Amalekites and totally destroy *all* that belongs to them. Do not spare them; put to death men and women, children and infants, cattle and sheep, camels and donkeys" (NIV, emphasis mine).

Destroy *all* that belongs to them, He said. God did not ask Saul for his opinion. God did not ask Saul if he had a better strategy or plan. God gave an instruction and expected his servant to carry it out. However, in verses 8–9, Saul decided he had a better plan. Saul did what he felt was right. He did exactly what looked good and made sense in his mind. He was very proud of his accomplishment. Not only did Saul miss it on this one, but he allowed pride to cause him to boast about what he had done. He was completely blinded by pride. He didn't even realize he had done anything wrong. If you don't learn to die to self, pride will keep you from having a repentant heart and taking accountability for your actions (see 1 Samuel 15:20–21).

When asked about what he had done, not only did Saul not take responsibility, but he placed part of the blame on the soldiers. Who were the orders given to? The assignment was given to Saul. Saul, as the leader, was to instruct and lead the soldiers to do exactly what God said. No additions, no variations, no subtractions.

When he didn't, his disobedience caused everyone attached to him to fall into disobedience. As a result, God said he was sorry he had ever made Saul a king and rejected him (1 Samuel 15:22–26). When I read this, I immediately repented and wept before God. All this time, I really believed I was right. I believed I had a right. I didn't understand the cost of my disobedience. My leader was carrying out orders from their leader, which came from the direction of the Holy Spirit, and I in my little mind thought it was okay to question the orders. Who in the world did I think I was? All I had to do was fall into position and carry out my part of the assignment. That's it, nothing more. It didn't cost me anything, so what was my issue? It's very difficult to minister to or lead anyone who believes they are above the authority of Christ. It's even more difficult to minister and lead when you are the one who believes you are above authority. My rebellion was like the sin of witchcraft and divination. Through my rebellion, I had also caused others to question authority. I had planted seeds of discord and didn't even know it. Lord, forgive me! Not my will but Your will be done.

Rebellion had been a part of who I was even as a child, especially during my preteen and teenage years. Mom said do this—I felt I had a right to say no. Mom said don't do this—I felt I had a right to do it anyway. I fought everything. I questioned everything. I could never simply obey. Mom would drop me off at the bus stop to go to school, and instead of going to school, I got right back off at another stop to go do whatever *I* wanted to do. I could never lay aside what I thought was right and receive wisdom, experience, and love. I was stubborn, hardheaded, and disrespectful, and no one could stop me. I knew what was right, yet the decisions I made cost me time, integrity, and valuable relationships. I look back on the lessons I could have learned by just listening rather than having to go through the experience. I was a confused teenage girl who resisted authority and guidance in every way. I was a great student and wonderful friend, but I was toxic to myself and my future.

I understand this is a phase that many of us go through and eventually we wake up and see how dumb we are. It didn't matter what people said to me; I had to hear it from God through His word. It convicted me so deeply that I couldn't do anything but lay down and die to myself. My self was dangerous and destructive. I had to learn how to obey and submit to authority. I had to learn to support my leadership without fighting, questioning, or criticizing their every move. I had to learn to be quiet and listen. Is it easy? Absolutely not, but it's so necessary.

I am so grateful that my leader at that time constantly reminded me that obedience is better than sacrifice. He did not let up and he did not compromise. Saul compromised. He said he was afraid of the men and gave them what they wanted. Leaders, this is a trap we cannot fall into. When people begin to complain, it can become so tempting to smite the rock (Numbers 20:8–13). We can become so blinded by what we see and what we believe to be right that we forget about the original assignment. Leaders, no matter what, stick to the original plan God gave you. Along the way you may have to make some adjustments, but stay focused on the end goal, the vision. Die to yourself, your plans, and your desires. Am I saying that you can't dream, you can't plan, you can't go after the things you desire? Of course not! What I am saying is allow the Holy Spirit to be your guide and teacher. Allow those things He desires for your life to become your desires. Allow His plans to become *the* plan for your life.

> But seek first his kingdom and his righteousness, and all these things will be given to you as well. — Matthew 6:33, NIV

5. Understand that you are not the only one who can lead

Your ideas are not always the best ideas. You can't fulfill a God-given vision alone, therefore God sends you a team of people who will partner with you in fulfilling the vision and everyone wins. There are two valuable points I have learned along my journey. The first is that we as leaders must

Empower one another. Everyone has a gift. God has given each of you a gift. Use it to help each other. This will show God's loving favor (1 Peter 4:10). When you empower one another, everyone operates and functions according to what they have been given (Ephesians 4:11–20).

Teach responsibility and accountability. Leaders, you can teach, pour into others, be a model, provide resources and literally set others up for success, but without responsibility and accountability, the spiritual and physical well-being and growth of the congregation will become an unrealistic expectation for the senior leaders to bear.

LEADERSHIP NUGGET:

Lose the part of yourself that causes you to fight against vision, purpose, assignment, and authority.

Some people see dying to self as losing your self-identity. Well, in a way, it is. You must lose the part of yourself that causes you to fight against vision, purpose, assignment, and authority, the part that won't let you be an overcomer and move beyond your past. That part of you must die so you may live in Christ the way God designed you to live: with purpose and value.

Dying to self has made me a better leader and allowed me to move confidently in the areas I have been anointed for. Leaders, be confident in God in you and take pride in everything you do, yet remember that detrimental and puffed-up pride has no place in the life of a believer. Die to self, remain humble, and take on the character and mind of Christ. It's just so much easier.

WHAT WE LEARNED: GOD'S EYES

In order to live, you can't be afraid to die. Living isn't really living until you're willing to die for something more important than yourself. You'll only experience true freedom when you're willing to let go of the things that have no stake in your eternal future.

Pride is the enemy of progression. Pride is subtle. It never comes at you directly. It always sneaks in through the guise of well-meaning sacrifice. In the end, God is not interested in a sacrifice that doesn't involve the death of self.

His voice must become the only voice. Many voices will speak to you during your leadership journey. They will speak with reason and passion. They will be persuasive. Every voice, however, is not of God. When God's voice becomes the preeminent voice in your hearing, it drowns out everything that is not like Him. Verbatim compliance is the only acceptable course of action.

Your discernment must become keener. Clarity, clarity, clarity! In order to hear the voice of the Lord over all other voices, you'll need to quiet the noise. Don't be afraid to shut everything down and find a place of solitude to hear clearly. It's better to take a few moments to find the flashlight than to stumble around in the dark, knocking everything over.

You become a usable vessel. It is often said that a full vessel cannot be used. When you die to self, you pour out everything that is not like the Father and make room for Him to use you as He sees fit. It's never about what you want—it's always about what He wants! When you want what He wants, He grants you your heart's desires.

REFLECTION
Questions for Discussion

1. What does "die to self" mean to you?

2. What does pride mean to you, both good pride and destructive pride?

3. In what areas of your life does pride remain?

4. What are you most afraid of losing as a result of dying to yourself?

5. In your own words, define rebellion.

6. In what areas of your life does rebellion remain?

7. What do brokenness and wholeness look like to you?

8. Are you willing to fully undergo the necessary process of dying to self, becoming broken in order to be whole?

Chapter 3
SUFFERING AND GAIN

HIS EYES

> So that [the genuineness] of your faith may be
> tested, [your faith which is infinitely more precious
> than the perishable gold which is tested and purified
> by fire. [This proving of your faith is intended] to
> redound to [your] praise and glory and honor when
> Jesus Christ (the Messiah, the Anointed One) is
> revealed. —1 Peter 1:7, AMPC

Suffering! Ponder and calmly think of that! Suffering is painful, costly, slow, and transformative. It is unavoidable and necessary, and without it, I would not have grown. When I started out in my walk with God, there was love, joy, and peace. I was like a newborn baby who hadn't lived enough life to know any better. Call it immaturity, but I was just happy to be in the presence of God and His people. As I grew in the Lord and took on greater leadership roles, the degree of suffering intensified. It's one thing to sacrifice a meal for a mandated fast, but it's completely mind-blowing to have your entire world turned upside down by the demands of ministry. If sacrifice is about forgoing things that would otherwise make your life more pleasant, then suffering is the process of enduring the sacrifice.

Before we really got started in ministry, I witnessed enough to know it would be demanding. I read the scriptures. I observed the lives of leaders in ministry and leadership. In some cases, I served as the sounding board for some of my leaders as they confided their deepest pains and hurts to me. I often thought, why me? Who am I? What makes me qualified? In some ways I naively believed I was equipped with some special knowledge that would insulate me from personally experiencing the realities of suffering. Man, was I so very wrong! If anything, I found out that God gave me a preview of what He was going to take me through. Truthfully, having insider knowledge made me excited, angry, and depressed all at the same time. I liken the experience to that of Jesus in the Garden of Gethsemane—with full knowledge of the plan for man's redemption, He faced the reality of His human emotions, knowing the path before Him would ultimately lead to suffering and death under the most severe and inhumane conditions.

In 1996, I was born again. The period from 1996 until 2012 was preparation for suffering to come. My family experienced multiple economic hardships, my dad (with whom I had only recently reconciled) died unexpectedly, and my military career kept me separated from my family for months. It was tough, but in spite of it all, the suffering was bearable. I was growing in ministry— personally and professionally. A growing child, although he experiences growth pains, doesn't wish he would stop growing. He endures because he knows that when it's over, he will be taller, faster, and better than he was before. That's how I viewed it. It was part of the process. I was growing spiritually, and isn't that what it's all about, anyway? Besides, it doesn't last forever, right?

In 2013, my wife and I founded Sure Foundation Kingdom Ambassadors in southeastern Virginia. Some might have believed we had arrived. For 17 years we had served faithfully in every ministry where we were assigned, both domestically and internationally. We never sat idle. We produced fruit. We discipled. We supported our leadership. We gave of our time, talent, and treasure. We sacrificed. We suffered. While our "elevation" to "pastoral" leadership appeared to be the reward for faithful service, it was really a death sentence.

I know this sounds cynical, but wasn't the cross the same thing for Jesus? Every experience prior to this moment was preparation for the suffering to come. We started with only a few in our home. By faith and the unction of the Holy Spirit, we moved into a hotel conference room. Shortly afterward, I received a military assignment that left my wife to navigate the ministry alone until my return (and she did this while managing our home of five). I returned from my assignment and reengaged only to experience a mini-stroke a few short weeks later. This moment dramatically changed the trajectory of our lives spiritually, physically, mentally, emotionally, and financially. It was only a preview of suffering to come. I began to question, Am I really built for this? God simply reminded me, as He did the apostle Paul in 2 Corinthians 12:9, "My grace is sufficient." Although this brought comfort, it didn't change my reality.

The years of intense suffering manifested between 2018 and 2019. I experienced stress and depression in unhealthy amounts. I was scatterbrained and unfocused, and lacked passion. I was reactive. I was in distress. My family was in distress. My relationships were in distress. My finances were in distress. The ministry was in distress. I was deeply immersed in the well-known axiom of "broke, busted, and disgusted." I had given everything to the ministry, and it had taken everything. I was completely spent. I felt like a failure as a man in all the roles that accompany the responsibility of manhood. I felt alone and defeated. Worse yet, people were looking to me for leadership when leading was the last thing I wanted to do. It was clear: I couldn't continue on this way. I needed soul care. I needed rest. I needed to reset. Here's what I learned:

1. When you're lost—stop!

The best thing you'll ever do as a leader is to rest, refresh, and reset. You cannot successfully lead anyone anywhere when you are lost yourself. Honestly, I didn't know how to just stop! It took some strong urging from the Holy Spirit and my wife to convince me. It was the best thing I could have ever done. Momentum going in the wrong direction will never get you to your destination. In fact, it might even be detrimental (you could be driving straight for a cliff)! Here is a simple tool to help when life gets overwhelming:

S Stop. Get quiet. Too much noise only confuses the situation.

T Take inventory. Ask, "Did I pick up/put down something I needed/didn't need?"

O Orient yourself. Make a shift. Determine whether it's the vehicle or you that needs to change direction.

P Proceed again. Don't get caught in the trap of fear that prevents moving forward again.

2. Remember that you're never alone

As bad as my suffering appeared, I had to remember it was only a shadow. No situation is ever as bad as it appears. Psalms 23 illustrates the transitory walk through the valley of the shadow of death. In other words, no matter how dark it may be darkness always disappears when light appears. I also had to remember that in my darkness I was being guided by the Shepherd's staff and protected by the Shepherd's rod. It is easy to become disillusioned while leading in ministry. It's hard. It's demanding. It requires everything you have. You will often give more than everyone else, and that, sets you apart whether you like it or not. Leadership is lonely, but with God, you are never alone.

Her Eyes

> You are not only to put your trust in Him, but you are to suffer for Him also. —Philippians 1:29, NLV

Suffering is something that we will all experience. We look at that word, *suffering*, and we think of doom and defeat, and often lose hope. But through all my sufferings, I can only say, "this is good, and this is necessary." Our ministry began with our family of eight and a family of two more in our living room. Little by little, people came, and people also left. Yet, things were moving quickly. Our faith was increasing. Nothing about this journey was easy, nor did

I expect it to be easy, but I maintained hope. Within five years of beginning the ministry, we purchased a building with land and started a Christian school. Everything appeared to be going well. However, beyond the pulpit, only a few knew of the real struggles and sufferings.

If we read through the book of Acts, we notice the sufferings that came to the early Christians, and particularly to Peter and John (Acts 4:3), Paul (Acts 14:19), Stephen (7:54–60), and James (Acts 12:1–2). If we are Christians, we can expect to suffer simply because we said yes to the call. The more determined we are to be followers of Christ, the more we must be prepared to suffer for Him.

At first, suffering was hard to understand. In the back of mind, I thought, Lord, I have served faithfully. I have submitted to my leaders. I have given greatly of my time, talent, and treasure. I always go above and beyond and never expect anything in return. I love, and I live a life that exemplifies my love for God and God's people. I pray, I teach, I preach, I fast, I worship . . . What is all this about? What is going on? I felt as though I was in a bad movie and couldn't wait for the credits to start rolling. We had financial issues like we had never imagined experiencing. Every month we asked the question, do we close the doors of the church and school or do we sell our home and start over?

No one knew that everything was coming out of our pockets, and I do mean everything. No one knew that we were paying payroll out of our pockets because tuition was either unpaid or late. No one knew that the mortgage on the building was coming out of our pockets. No one knew that our children were suffering with us. I was not ashamed, because we had done nothing wrong. We were great stewards over everything that we were blessed with, we just didn't have enough. I just did not feel as though anyone could help me in the way I needed to be helped. In my season of need and weakness, God's grace became my strength.

Her Strength: Going through with Grace

Grace, which comes from the Greek New Testament word *charis*, is God's unmerited favor.

Webster's New World College Dictionary provides this theological definition of grace: "The unmerited love and favor of God toward human beings; divine influence acting in a person to make the person pure, morally strong; the condition of a person brought to God's favor through this influence; a special virtue, gift, or help given to a person by God."

The first week of May 2018 hit me in the deepest part of my soul. This was something I could have never imagined would happen. I was in shock, and physically exhausted. My heart ached like it had never ached before. But there was a supernatural strength and peace that overtook me. It was now Sunday. Word had gotten out about what had happened, and someone had to make a decision: I could sit here in this house dwelling on the events that had just taken place, or I could get up and keep pressing. I got my girls and we drove to church. After praise and worship went forth, I asked the congregation to take a chair and let's go outside. I didn't have any notes, just a single word and a passage from the Holy Spirit. I spoke a word from the depths of my belly with such power and anointing right there in the parking lot. The message was titled, "Don't Allow Your Response in the Valley to Hinder Your Next Mountaintop Experience." I could've smitten the rock. I could have run to the cave. I could have pleaded for God to take this thorn from my side. I was hurting in a deep place, yet I knew I would get through this and I could keep standing.

I am telling you this was like a bad movie that I wanted to walk out on. But there was something on the inside of me that pushed me even harder. There was a fight in me that would not allow me to quit. I was not naive about the natural losses, but in the spirit, I only saw my gain. This made me want to fight even more.

On Mother's Day of that year, just a few weeks later, I was asked to minister at my father's church in Detroit, Michigan. I drove for thirteen hours alone with my daughter. I preached about women being empowered by God, all while enduring a gut-wrenching feeling of helplessness. Only my mother knew everything that was going on. After service, we all went out to dinner. While we were waiting to be called to our table, I shared with my father what happened, and I could see the hurt and genuine concern on his face as he fought back tears. He pressed through dinner, but after I returned home, he called me every day to make sure everything was okay. I didn't know that was the last time I would see him alive.

In October of 2018, my father transitioned home. Besides my husband, he was the only spiritual counselor I had. There was no one I could go to and ask for prayer and spiritual advice, and no one who believed in or truly supported anything I was doing that was connected to God and ministry. My earthly father was not perfect and he certainly made mistakes, but he loved God and loved and served God's people until he couldn't anymore. I didn't cry until they closed the casket for the final time. I only rejoiced in the comfort of knowing where he now rested. Within that year alone, I had experienced emotional, physical, mental, financial, and spiritual losses. They all hit me very hard, one after the other.

Some of you may be asking what happened. As a leader, you will learn that not all testimonies are for you to share. Although we overcome by hearing the testimonies of others, there is also an accountability and responsibility for experiences, especially when they involve others. I can tell my part and how it affected me, but I respect and honor those who also experienced the same hurt, to allow them the time to share their portion of the testimony. Through it all, know this: it's only through God's grace and strength that any of us have been able to endure.

The following months were full of stress and strain on my marriage, the ministry, and my family. I continued to preach, teach, worship, and lead. I was dying a slow spiritual death. I allowed myself to become empty, dangerously empty! I felt unheard, disrespected, overlooked, under appreciated, and alone. I became bitter, irritated, and frustrated with the people around me. I had been in ministry for so long that I knew how to go through the motions. However, on the inside I didn't care if I ever stepped into another church in my life. I wasn't giving up on God, but my heart began to harden toward the people. I tried to keep smiling and be an encouragement to others, but the truth is I was in need of true encouragement, refreshing, and refueling myself. Just as I reached a point when I could actually process and grieve over every event that had taken place, the very same thing happened again. I had to pick myself up and keep going.

Leaders, I had to be delivered. My frustration, my emotions, my lack of ability to refresh and refuel left me empty, resentful, and running on residue. I was unhealthy and unusable. It was time for a reset! After wrestling, do we continue or do we stop? Do we continue, but shift the way we are functioning, and what does that look like? In October of 2019, we announced we were going on sabbatical. Leaders, sometimes you have to stop and refresh.

3. Know when it's time to stop and refresh

It's important to recognize when you have come to a point that if you continue in the state you are in, everything around you becomes tainted and unhealthy. *Danger!* And *damaging!* So, stop! Remove yourself and get it together. In your pain, you begin to hurt others who have nothing to do with your situation. Get out of the way. Get yourself together and hit the reset button. After so many miles, you must change out the oil in your car and get an engine flush or you will cause damage to your engine and create friction and unnecessary heat. Go refresh your oil. Take care of your spirit and heal.

In many ways, it was very easy to feel like a failure, but I continued to hear the Holy Spirit say, "No, Daughter, this is your gain. This is your opportunity to move into something greater. This is freedom!" Hallelujah! I begin to reflect on the closed doors, the losses, and the sacrifices, and I chose to only focus on the good. I was reminded of my prayers to enlarge my area of influence and employment opportunities came immediately. I was reminded of my prayers to help me to break out of my state of wilderness rotation, of repetition and regurgitation, and suddenly opportunities for speaking engagements became available. Doors were closing, but others were opening that I was not even aware of yet. Without the sacrifice of letting go, I left no room for the overflow. I was okay with it all. I felt free and unweighted. This was good. God's grace kept me and every sacrifice became a great gain.

LEADERSHIP NUGGET

Without the sacrifice of letting go,
there is no room for overflow.

4. Know when it's time to let it all go

> Now that we know what we have—Jesus, this great High Priest with ready access to God—let's not let it slip through our fingers. We don't have a priest who is out of touch with our reality. He's been through weakness and testing, experienced it all— all but the sin. So let's walk right up to him and get what he is so ready to give. Take the mercy, accept the help. —Hebrews 4:14–16, MSG

Embrace the closed doors and trust there are other opportunities available for you. The moment I let certain things go, not only physically, but mentally and emotionally, I began to feel the weights removed. God began to open doors and make connections I could have never made remaining where I was. Do not be afraid to close your doors; maybe God needs you to be flexible and available to move when He calls. Don't be afraid to disconnect from certain organizations and positions, God may be redeeming your time. During this time of reset, I also stepped down from positions and responsibilities within the community. Don't get me wrong—I was very passionate about everything I was doing and they were all good and all a part of my ministry. However, it was time for me to let it go. Don't be afraid to look different and be bold enough to be different. When you decide to make room for your increase, don't feel you have to explain a whole lot to anyone. Just trust that God knows best. Whatever you believe is good, God has better. *Make room for your increase.*

> I assure you and most solemnly say to you, unless a grain of wheat falls into the earth and dies, it remains alone [just one grain, never more]. But if it dies, it produces much grain and yields a harvest. —John 12:24, AMP

5. Practice self-care

I can't close out this chapter without stressing the importance of recognizing when you need help, but being humble enough to go get help. Our family recognized we could no longer manage all of the stress on our own and remain healthy, so we sought out family therapy during our sabbatical and we have loved every moment. There is finally someone I can talk to who knows nothing about me. Although God's grace has, and continues to, give me strength, His wisdom tells me the importance of wholeness. Leaders, therapy and counseling for yourself is needed and necessary. The weight and responsibility that you bear can only be understood by another leader. Don't suffer in silence; use every resource that's available to you. You matter!

WHAT WE LEARNED GOD'S EYES

God prepares you for what He is going to take you through. God always gives us little tests and small victories along the way. Each test becomes progressively more difficult because it is ultimately leading us to the fulfillment of His greater purpose. You don't go to a gym and immediately expect to lift the heaviest weight. Instead, you gradually work up to it. In the same fashion, God doesn't send us an army to defeat—He sends us sheep to keep and to tend to. He'll occasionally throw in a bear and a lion to defeat in order to build our confidence. When we least expect it, He'll send us a Goliath to establish His purpose. Don't quit before the great reveal—it's coming!

Be willing to let it all go in order to make room for increase. Like the rich young ruler found in the Bible, the same is true: you will not have God's best until you're willing to let go of the rest. As cliché as it sounds, there is no substitute for total relinquishment. God requires everything: heart, soul, mind, and strength. It's nonnegotiable. The greatest suffering (usually self-induced) is often experienced when we continue to fight for our "rights." God is essentially saying, "You keep fighting for your one cow, when I own the cattle on a thousand hills." When we let go of what we think is important, God gives us what really is important and in alignment with His will.

Your strength and peace are in God. This statement could stand right here. Paul's letter to the Philippians reminded them not to be anxious. Suffering, at its outset, is uncomfortable. By definition and design, it is supposed to be. Regardless of how it feels, it is important to remember God never fails. It is during the most difficult times when we must rehearse God's resumé so that we may remember every victory won, every foe defeated, and every valley traversed. In all of it, He never leaves, never forsakes, nor does He ever lose!

The fulfillment of purpose is found in individual suffering. Suffering whittles away everything that doesn't belong and shapes us into what we are. Notice—we did not say "what we become." When God made each of us, He made us unique, with purpose. It is already in there! Unfortunately, distractions get in the way. Suffering is God's way of removing the unnecessary in order to release the extraordinary.

Suffering is the removal of self from the equation for God's greater purpose. God allows suffering so "His power is made perfect in weakness" (2 Corinthians 12:19, ASV). He uses suffering to strengthen our trust in His divine power to deliver us in any situation. Does that mean everything in the physical realm does an immediate 180-degree turn? Sometimes, but not usually. What we learned is that we can have a complete paradigm shift concerning our situation. Instead of viewing it from a "woe is me" perspective, we now see it as God's way of perfecting us for His greater purpose—to impact the world for His glory!

REFLECTION
Questions for Discussion

1. What do you feel was your greatest moment of suffering?

2. What did you learn from your suffering?

3. How do you believe God prepared you for your suffering?

4. What was your gain?

5. While you were going through this process, what was your posture?

6. If you could share some insight about what it means to suffer for Christ, what would it be?

Chapter 4

BEFORE WE WERE PASTORS, WE WERE HUSBAND AND WIFE

I am convinced: everything I need to know about life and how to live it (and not live it) can be found in the first three chapters of the Bible. Yet, armed with this infallible knowledge, I can honestly say I still manage to get it wrong more times than I'm willing to admit. This is particularly true in the area of balance. As a general rule, I tend to be an "all-in or not at all" kind of guy. Believe me when I tell you, this viewpoint wreaks havoc with relationships, commitments, and execution. To say the "struggle is real" is an understatement! This has been true of my ministry efforts to the Body of Messiah and to my family, and in particular, to my wife. In my humble opinion, I believe there are no two stronger polarizing forces in the life of the ministry leader than these—serving God and serving people. But how do you reconcile the two without neglecting one and performing an injustice to the other? How do you maintain balance when the pull is so great? Now, that is the question.

Husband: Before We Are Pastors, We Are Husband and Wife!

> Therefore a man shall leave his father and his mother and shall become united and cleave to his wife, and they shall become one flesh. —Genesis 2:24, AMPC

When my wife and I first met, I was not looking for a relationship.

I didn't see us married. It wasn't love at first sight. In fact, we often tell the story of how she pursued me. Fortunately, I came around. I fell deeply in love with the woman I am privileged to call my best friend, partner, and wife. While she doesn't complete me (only God can do that), she complements me. The longer we are together, the more I note the similarities in our thoughts and actions. We are truly becoming one in Christ. We didn't enter into the covenant relationship ideally. We both came from maritally challenged (divorced) homes. We were promiscuous. We were teenaged parents from a major metropolitan city. We had a lot of baggage. The odds certainly were not in our favor.

Our new life in Christ only amplified the need to unpack those bags. Instead, as a young and newly minted Christian, my zeal and commitment to the "work of the ministry" set the stage for how I compartmentalized life—at home, at work, at church, and in general. "God, family, and then everything else," they said. Little did I know this tiny philosophical cliché would become one of the greatest landmines in my covenant relationship with my wife. Believe it or not, it happens more often than you might imagine. What begins as small adjustments and minor discomforts in the name of ministry soon becomes all-out unhealthy sacrifices of time, talent, treasure, and yes, relationships. I met the needs at church, I met the needs at work, and I totally disregarded my love's needs. It doesn't happen overnight. It grows quietly with time and added leadership responsibility. It's subtle. The demands of everything else became priority. I reasoned, "She'll understand. We're in this together. She gets it. She knows the demand." And she did—for a while.

For years, I placed her needs on the back burner for the needs of work and ministry. I shouldn't have been surprised when she no longer sat quietly. I should have seen it coming. I should have heard her screams. In retrospect, I did, but I was out of balance. Worse yet, I was conflicted. I needed to learn how to give in to her voice because she was right, but the demands of ministry were at an all-time high. I should have listened and heeded. Instead, I pressed on. She got louder. I became frustrated. Her words became piercing. I became resentful and angry. Not at her—I was angry because I didn't know how to help her, I didn't know how to keep ministering to others when I was failing at home, and I was hurting. We were divided. I believe this can be attributed to my failure to listen and/or respond appropriately to my wife's heart during pivotal moments in our relationship. Here, I'll list some of the most important things I learned.

1. Listen

Men, if there's one thing I want to impart—one skill I would admonish you to hone—it's the art of listening. Admittedly, I must work at it. Believe me when I tell you, it's hard work, but it's worth it. I don't believe there is a woman on the planet who doesn't want a man who listens. I'm not just talking about listening to the words she says, but listening to her heart. The heart of the wife has a unique frequency that is masterfully tuned to her husband's ear. The concerns of life create interference and it's important for us (men) to remove anything that creates that "noise." This noise can be anything from career, to education, to ministry, and even children.

Side note for the wives (and this is going to sound harsh, but it's not): Your husband didn't marry any of these other things—career, education, ministry, children, etc.—he married you. All of these accentuate and complement your union, and while each has its level of importance and priority, none of them should ever disrupt the frequency of your heart toward your husband. Remember, jobs will change, children will "cleave and leave," but your husband has vowed to be there no matter what.

Don't let your frequency become "white noise" in his ear. He will eventually tune it out.

Here's the unfortunate issue: husbands often hear the voices of their wives rather than their hearts. By the time they hear her voice, it's often too late. The window of opportunity for peaceful resolve has passed. Trust me—I'm an expert in this area (and not by choice, either)! It's important to hear her heart before you hear her voice.

Too many times, my wife was speaking to me with the "still quiet voice of her heart" and I missed its sound because I allowed the interference of life's vicissitudes to tune her out.

2. Respond

After you have heard her heart, it's paramount to respond accordingly. I'm not talking about words full of unwanted solutions or well-meaning promises. Instead, your (and my) response must be with action. There might be good (even great) reasons you respond slowly. In the end—let's be honest—it's a well-crafted excuse to justify inaction. I can assure you that none of the reasons you come up with matter. One of the greatest mistakes I have made throughout my life, in marriage, and in ministry is not responding when my wife's heart was speaking. I had to learn (and I am still learning) how to remove the interference. There are three ways to defeat the interference hindering you from hearing her frequency:

Go higher. If you ever pay attention to cell phone towers, you'll notice the antennas are positioned high. The reason is obvious: up high, fewer items block the path of the signal (i.e., trees, buildings, etc.). The more you develop your relationship with God, the higher you go. In other words, when your concerns are focused on the cares of this world (see Mark 4:19), you experience blockages in your productivity, your relationships, and your fruitfulness. The higher you go in God, the better you will hear your spouse.

Amplify. Just as height helps optimize an antenna's signal path, the amount of power behind the signal amplifies it. The stronger the signal, the less likely it will be overcome by interference. A strong signal cuts through the "noise" or distractions that prevent good communication and connection. The more time you spend with God in His word and in prayer, the stronger you become. You clear a path for the sound of His voice (and the voice of your spouse) to be heard despite the noise surrounding it.

Synchronize. Every cell phone that transmits a signal has a unique identifier. It helps the regulating authority quickly identify any device that may be operating outside of its parameters, as well as connect with the intended party. In order to communicate with another device, both devices need to operate on the same frequency. In other words, they must sync up. My wife and I have different "frequencies"; yet, when we get on God's carrier signal, our individual signals become one in Him, and we hear each other's hearts clearly.

3. Get rid of the compartments

Balance in ministry is often defined as "God, family, and then everything else." I'm going to step out on a limb here. I think this is a misguided manmade paradigm. In fact, I'm inclined to believe it's a false narrative Christendom has come up with to exalt personal agendas in the name of God while neglecting the relationships that reflect His personality, character, and makeup. Whoa! I know. It's a heavy statement that is sure to ruffle some feathers. But stick with me for a second. What if the definition is wrong? God never said to compartmentalize purpose. Instead, He created humanity to live wide open and unconstrained. He created us to be fully engaged in relationship with Him and with all of creation. Compartmentalizing, while helpful in managing resources, can be restrictive and unhelpful when building meaningful relationships with others. When we as men operate in this fashion, especially in leadership, we create and foster constrained cultures that make what we do of no effect.

4. Learn to surrender

One of the toughest challenges in ministry and life is learning to surrender. Let's face it: Men just don't surrender. Men would just as soon die as surrender. We will allow our arm to be twisted out of its socket for the sake of not granting our opponent the satisfaction of victory over us. I had to relearn that my wife, my love, was not my opponent. I had to remember that we are one. Unbalanced ministry will pit you against your loved ones and create division in your home and in everything else you touch. Getting balanced meant surrendering my will, first to the Father, then to my wife. Many men will find that surrender is hard, but it is very possible.

The apostle Paul writes:

Husbands, love your wives, as Christ loved the church and gave himself up for her, that he might sanctify her, having cleansed her by the washing of water with the word, so that he might present the church to himself in splendor, without spot or wrinkle or any such thing, that she might be holy and without blemish. —Ephesians 5:25–27, ESV

My wife, my marriage, is illustrative of my responsibility to lay down my life for her. I have had to learn that my opinions, ideas, and goals are always the things that bring out her very best.

Before children, before ministry, before anything else—there was (and still is) this special something between us. It is the flame to which the proverbial moth is drawn, and I am still drawn to that flame nearly three decades later! It hasn't always been this way. In fact, there were some moments in our relationship when the flame was nothing more than a flicker.

LEADERSHIP NUGGET

Life, work, family, ministry—all of these will work overtime to extinguish your flame. Always remember, before you are anything else, you are husband and wife. Guard your marriage and protect it with your life!

Her Eyes

In church we are all taught "God, family, then ministry." When God is first, everything else is supposed to fall into place. But what does the Bible say? Your family is absolutely your first ministry: "If anyone does not know how to manage his own family, how can he take care of God's church?" (1 Timothy 3:5, NIV). Totally agree! However, what happens to the family of leaders when there's a demand in the ministry? What happens when no one else is there, but it still has to get done? The leaders end up picking up what everyone else misses. And guess what? Your children get dragged into the duties as well. How many times have you said, "No, we can't," or "Not this time" to a request of your children because of a ministry commitment? How many events or activities have you missed because of your commitment to ministry? However, we will discuss more about the children in the next chapter.

Wife: Before We Were Pastors, We Were Husband and Wife!

> However, each one of you also must love his wife as he loves himself, and the wife must respect her husband. —Ephesians 5:33, NIV

Submission. Yes, I know, ladies. You're probably so tired of hearing that word, *submission.* Then the question arises, what if I'm not married—does this still apply? Is the concept or principle of submission dated based on our current culture? If I'm the main financial provider of my house, do I still have to submit to my husband? I will submit to you that, in a marriage or any covenant relationship, submission to leadership is still a Godly principle and heartbeat of God. I agree that with all the opportunities and empowerment that we as women have today, submission can be a hard pill to swallow. Yes, we can do almost anything a man can do, just as well if not better in some cases. We hold the same degrees and have some of the same skills as men. However, I have to ask the question, what was God's original plan? Did His plan for us change, or did we adjust and adapt to our circumstances in order to survive?

In 1979–1980, my parents were divorced and my mother raised my brother and I. Like most homes with a single mother, we had our struggles, but my mother was very strong and determined to succeed. As a result, she taught me independence and survival. I witnessed my mother survive on one income to support the three of us. We did not go without. Our car was never repossessed, our utilities were never cut off, we were never without food, we were never without shoes or clothes to wear, we went to school every

42

day, and we lived in a suburb of Detroit, Michigan, in our three-bedroom home. In addition to raising two children, my mother also continued her education and obtained her master's in education. I stand here today and shout to the world how proud I am of my mother for being such an example of strength in my life. However, in all of the independence, I did not understand the importance of submission. I wasn't taught how to be a wife. This I learned through another kind of strength, the strength and love of God.

> The more I fell in love with God, the more I fell in love with my husband. The more I submitted to God, the easier it was to submit to my husband.
> —Tamara Nichols

Married women, please respect your husband at all times. I speak from the experience of what an immature wife with an untamed tongue can do to the heart and spirit of her husband. Early in my marriage, I thought my feelings and opinions mattered more than the pride of my husband. I was wrong! Very wrong! So, what happens when you just don't agree? If the congregation can sense there is a lack of unity and harmony among the leadership, it makes it challenging to minister effectively and expect everyone else to move as a unified body. There have been many times when I simply did not agree with how certain things were taught or handled and I remained silent.

My desire, and I would like to believe it is every married woman's desire for her home, is that my husband will lead and be the spiritual head of our home. In order for him to fulfill that role, I must stay out of his way and allow him to lead. I must allow him to do what he was created to do. If I want him to lead, I can't take away his voice as a leader with my own overbearing voice. I can't try to control every situation. I must submit. Please don't close the book. Stay with me and continue reading.

As the pastor's wife, I haven't always seen everything the way my husband does, and I'm not expected to. He has a view and I have a view, but it's how I responded in those moments that has made the difference. I had to go back to why God created this order and how easy it became to submit to my husband for the last twenty-five years. I remembered that once I began to allow God to do what needed to be done in me, I began to love Him as my Father even more. The more I fell in love with Christ, the more I fell in love with my husband. I had a hunger and a thirst to know more about Christ. As I learned more about Christ, His word began to teach me about me. The word began to teach me how to be His daughter, how to be a godly woman, and how to be a wife. Jesus gave up his life in exchange for the life of his bride. In Ephesians 5:21, Paul tells us all to submit to one another. He goes even further and says, "You wives must submit to your husbands' leadership in the same way you submit to the Lord. . . And you husbands, show the same kind of love to your wives as Christ showed to the Church when he died for her" (v. 22, 25, TLB).

Before I Was My Husband's Wife, I Was God's Daughter

However, balance is key! I will say this, submission can also become a hindrance if we do not fully understand the heart of God. In your submission, remember that God also had a plan and mandate for you and your life even before you were formed in your mother's womb. Wives, always remember, before you were his wife, you were His daughter, created with a purpose. Know your purpose, have a vision for yourself, and pursue it.

Your identity is in Christ, not in your occupation or your social, economic, marital, or parental status. All of these will vary and change. But your status as a daughter of the King of Kings will never change. There are some things God calls you to do alone, there are things you will accomplish as a couple, and there are things you will only accomplish with a team. Learn how to discern when and what so you do not put a wedge between you and your husband creating division and discord.

Here are a few steps that helped me understand submission in a healthy way so we could both win. I pray they help you, too.

1. Learn how to love yourself first

With all your heart, all your soul, all your mind, and all your strength, don't let anything come between you and God. Yearn for God. Long to hear His voice. Put everything down, lay it all aside, and then allow Him to love on you. To wrap you in his arms. To protect you. To comfort you. To be your provider, your strength, your joy, your peace. In other words, allow God to fulfill every void in your life *first*. Then and only then can you truly love, honor, respect, and submit to another, including yourself.

2. Crucify your flesh, humble yourself, and live like Christ lives in you

Come to the realization that it is no longer just about you and what you want. You have entered into a covenant that requires some sacrifice.

> I have been crucified with Christ. It is no longer I who live, but Christ who lives in me. And the life I now live in the flesh I live by faith in the Son of God, who loved me and gave himself for me. —Galatians 2:20, ESV

> Don't be selfish; don't try to impress others. Be humble, thinking of others as better than your-selves. Don't look out only for your own interests, but take an interest in others, too. —Philippians 2:3–4, NLT

This includes your husband's interests. You may not understand what he's talking about, you may not have any interest in what he's doing, but it's not always about you. Show your husband that you care about the things he cares about. Show him that he has your ear and he can come to you and bare his soul before you. Show him he can cry as a man and you will still love him as a man. Show him that you respect him and honor him as the Father's son and as your husband.

3. Learn how to submit to your husband

If you can't do this yet, go back and spend a bit more time on steps 1 and 2. If you're ready, read on.

Wives, in the same way submit yourselves to your own husbands so that, if any of them do not believe the word, they may be won over without words by the behavior of their wives, when they see the purity and reverence of your lives. —1 Peter 3:1–2, NIV

Wife, if you want your husband to lead, you must learn how to follow. No matter how long it takes for him to get there, you follow him, support him, push him, and encourage him, bringing out the very best in him. Going back to the idea of the independent woman, yes, we are perfectly capable of making money, climbing the corporate ladder, running corporations, and managing our own finances and homes. We can even change a tire, fix a toilet, build, create—the list goes on and on. But, *but then* . . . what have we left for our husbands to do? Where do they fit in? In many ways, our liberation has become our detriment.

Through our independence, we have stripped our husbands, and men in general, of their purpose as providers and leaders, but yet we still want them to lead. Women of God, we can't get mad at our husbands when we have so boldly shown them we don't need them, but they're nice to have around, like a pet. Submit and let them lead.

Lastly, wives, please:

4. Learn how to tame your tongue

> A worthy wife is a crown for her husband, but a disgraceful woman is like cancer in his bones. — Proverbs 12:4, NLT

> A wise woman builds her home, but a foolish woman tears it down with her own hands. —Proverbs 14:1, NLT

> Better to live on a corner of the roof than share a house with a quarrelsome wife. — Proverbs 21:9, NIV

> A quarrelsome wife is as annoying as constant dripping on a rainy day. —Proverbs 27:15, NLT

Be quiet! Sit down somewhere and just listen to the heart of your husband. God knew this would be an issue, so he provided you with examples of what your husband feels and thinks when you will not be quiet. Quit nagging and criticizing all the time. If your husband isn't coming straight home after work, don't automatically assume it's another woman. It could be that he just doesn't feel like hearing your mouth or he needs a moment to breathe in order to prepare and embrace what's waiting at home. So, show lovingkindness. Be a gentle heart. Smile when you see your love. Just as you respond in worship with your heart, respond to your husband the same way. Is submission easy? Is this something you learn overnight? No, but we can no longer say no one taught us how to be a wife. God, through His word, His Holy Spirit, and His love, has taught us everything we need for right living in every area of our lives.

WHAT WE LEARNED: GOD'S EYES

Let nothing interfere with the covenant, not even self. This cannot be overemphasized. People will come and go. Opportunities will present themselves and then disappear as quickly as they appeared. Resources will abound and they won't. Regardless of circumstances or personal feelings, sometimes all we will have is one another. Don't be so quick to kick your partner to the curb. God never intended for His covenant of marriage to be broken. The easiest way to defend your bond is to make up your mind in advance that nothing will separate you from your spouse except God and death.

Learn to flow as one. It gets easier, but you never arrive. It's work, work, and more work. The only way to really flow with one another is to find common ground in God's word and God's plan. Even when you disagree, you can always agree that He has the final say!

Submit to one another. Learning to let go of your personal will ultimately challenges you. Yet, until you and I do, we will never fully walk together in one accord. Submitting to one another in marriage, ministry, and life teaches us how to apply the practical wisdom of God in everyday living. Submitting to one another opens the door for deeper levels of commitment, intimacy, and fulfillment. Learning to submit to one another makes room for God to progress us to the levels and places he wants to bring us to.

There must be a healthy balance. When you're pursuing a healthy balance, communication is important. Learning to communicate effectively takes time, practice, and maturity. However, having someone of integrity to whom you both can talk to, give you spiritual insight, can be helpful for your relationship—something to consider.

REFLECTION
Questions for Discussion

1. Are you currently in ministry with your spouse?

2. Does surrendering your life mean giving up or losing your identity? Expound.

3. How do you balance ministry and marriage?

4. In your own words, define *submission.*

5. Do you find it challenging to submit to one another at times?

6. Is it challenging to flow as one in certain areas? Which areas, and why?

7. How important is it that both of you agree on situations related to family and ministry?

8. Do each of you have someone you can talk to outside of one another?

Chapter 5

THE BALANCING ACT
OF FAMILY AND MINISTRY

All right, friend. We are at the point of this journey where we feel compelled to take you a little deeper. It is a complicated issue and is, we believe, one of the most important hurdles in being a leader who wins. Learning how to balance family and ministry is both a science and an art. It's a science in understanding all the extremes, the elements, the relevance, and the importance of both, and an art in the creative ability to utilize all the elements with value and purpose but remain flexible, spontaneous, and accommodating. We were young leaders in ministry with three small children, and while our family was very important to us, we allowed ministry to take precedence. Were we wrong in what we were doing? Was our service and involvement wrong? No, we just did not balance home and ministry very well. This chapter will give you a glimpse of the views of dad, mom, and children in ministry to help show the necessity of good balance.

HIS EYES

Charity begins at home. –Terence (Publius Terentius Afer)

Dad: Don't Get So Busy Serving That You Forget to Serve at Home First

Let me begin by saying men love differently; not less, just differently. The way I serve my children is different from the way my wife serves them. I love my children very much. I always have and always will. I would exchange my life for theirs in a heartbeat. I have worked and sacrificed to give them stability and a childhood without the burdens I carried as a child. I never wanted them to experience life as I did—robbed of the opportunity to just be young. I have tried to instill godly character in them. I have supported them when I didn't agree. I've tried to be an example to them and to validate them and their gifts, talents, and abilities. Yet, I often feel as though I failed them as a dad. I failed to serve them well. It's a pain I can't shake. My naval career and personal ministry assignment have often created separation during times in their lives when they may have needed me most. In my efforts to make life better for them, I believe I may have done them an injustice. I would like to think I have a pretty good relationship with each of them, but I often feel like something is missing. Worse yet, I believe their relationship with God is not as strong because of me. For this, I have deep regret.

As a teenager, I was not ready for fatherhood. I had hopes. I had dreams. Poof! Gone! Here I was with a pregnant girlfriend and a baby on the way! Surely this wasn't happening right now! She was overjoyed. I, on the other hand, felt like I had been hit with a ton of bricks. Sure, I was happy. But happiness quickly melted under the immense heat of providing for a new life. It felt like a cruel joke. I had already spent most of my life filling in as the "man of the house."

I was just starting to feel like I could focus on having a life without having to worry about the needs of someone else, and now I was about to become the actual "man of the house." I grew up without my father in the home, and while my maternal grandfather did an absolutely wonderful job of helping to raise me, he was still Grandpa. He taught me about the principles and requirements expected of a man, but he didn't necessarily teach me how to be a dad.

There is an exchange that happens between a father and a child, and a son in particular, that resembles the act of passing a baton. I never got that baton pass. My father didn't. My maternal grandfather didn't. Neither of them ever had their fathers in their lives. All of us were raised by men who weren't our biological fathers. Sure, we knew how to work. We knew how to make a living, but making a living is not the same as making a family. None of us had a point of reference for that. Yet, there I was with the daunting task of finding and carrying a baton dropped by previous generations. I was determined not to have that stigma as the legacy I would leave my children. So I picked it up and I ran with it. I knew how to be responsible. Life taught me how to do that.

My girlfriend needed to finish high school. I needed to find full-time work to support my child. Dropping out of college was the solution. As a matter of course, I asked the mother of my child to marry me. It didn't take long to realize that I would have to do more than work minimum-wage jobs to take care of my fiancé and son. I found myself employed with the one organization I vowed I would never become affiliated with: the United States Navy. My wife and I married shortly thereafter and nine months later we were pregnant with a second child. Three years later, not too long after my wife and I gave our lives to God, we had our third child.

We were a financially strapped military family of five who would soon become heavily involved in ministry work. Needless to say, this was a recipe for failure. I worked to give them basic needs like shelter, food, and clothing, but I hadn't learned to give them the best of me. My career had me gone most of the time. Now, I was thrust into this new life in Christian ministry with no point of reference for how to protect my wife and children from the ills and demands that were inevitably commonplace. Here's what I've learned since then.

1. Focus on what matters

Nowadays I often ask myself, "Will any of it matter when I'm gone?" Reflecting on it all, I realize I haven't always put my family first. My great-grandmother was really the only example I had as a child with regard to ministry. She was a church mother and missionary. She was clearly a leader in her own right. She was the matriarch of the family. She was the glue that held us together. She was the one who helped me with my leg braces and took me for walks. She was the one who let me lick the bowl when she made sweet potato pie. She was the one I snapped green beans with. Whoever she was within the church congregation didn't matter to me. She was simply Great-Grandma. She died when I was five.

She possessed and was the very embodiment of a rare substance that, if it could be bottled, would make one an overnight success. I believe that substance is what some might call balance. Unfortunately, my family was never the same after she passed. She left behind an indelible impression of strength, selfless service, and leadership. Her commitment to her family and God's people was her legacy. It mattered to that little five-year-old boy! In truth, I know very little about what she gave to people at church. I do, however, remember what she did for me. People come and go, but family is forever.

2. Someone always pays

If you spend a few moments in conversation with anyone who has a family and serves in ministry leadership, you will very quickly discern an inexplicable heaviness of heart. Leadership in any organization or capacity is challenging, but the pull of leadership in ministry is a different dynamic altogether. Unfortunately, someone always pays, and family is usually that someone.

A fellow ministry leader said something that struck a major chord with me a couple of years ago. He said, "You can be a public success and a private failure." Whoa! Talk about a ton-of-bricks revelation. For over two decades, I have served in ministry in varying degrees of service and leadership. In fact, there isn't much I haven't done. I say this to my shame, and not my honor. To the onlooker, I have had some success. Many would laud these works as qualifications for ascension in ministry ranks, a payment of dues toward the hallmark of a leadership position, if you will. I would be grossly negligent if I didn't remind you of the cost of leadership—sacrifice is *always* an issue. I have sacrificed my family on the altar of "the work of the ministry" more times than I care to admit. Truthfully, it's a miracle my family even speaks to me when you factor in the dual sacrifice required of them as a result of my military service. Here was my biggest error: I assumed my family was just as committed as I was to the call. I could not have been more wrong!

3. There's a time for everything

> Balance is not something you find; it's something you create. —Jana Kingsford

There are some common misconceptions when it comes to ministry leaders. Contrary to popular belief, we don't sit around and study scripture all day. We don't spend all day locked in a room, praying. We haven't gone fishing. We aren't on the golf course. And, for the record, we don't spend all of our time eating fried chicken at parishioners' homes, either. In all seriousness, ministry leaders, in addition to their responsibility to attend to the spiritual oversight and instruction of those to whom they are called, spend a tremendous amount of time dealing with the wholeness issues (or the lack thereof) in people's lives. This often includes visiting, counseling, praying for and with people, resourcing, training, equipping, developing, coaching, fathering, mothering, and so on. Time usually doesn't readily avail itself for anything remotely resembling recreation. Even worse, we often fail to make time for our families. I can't tell you the number of times my wife made me take time off and I felt overwhelming guilt for doing so, especially with so many things left undone. Balance, as a leader, is something you must fight and contend for despite its clever elusiveness. It's something you have to create!

4. Stop adding to the plate

Anyone who leads and serves well knows the benefits of connecting with others. We glean and grow from the best that people have to offer. But leaders give more than they receive and take on more than they should. This includes the baggage and trash others leave behind. It's an occupational hazard.

Please hear me when I say this: this is not a complaint. I am stating a hard reality. Ministry is hard; it's messy; it's demanding. Here's the rub: it's all-consuming. In fact, we often bring home that trash and transmit it to our families. Before you get it twisted, I'm not saying we sit around the dinner table, talking about you. No, our actions, despondency, and distancing often separate us from our families as a way of protecting them from the landmines of ministry. In essence, we subconsciously add all the demands of ministry to the plate and remove our families from it altogether. A ministry leader's family ought to get the best from him or her, not what's left over (if anything at all). I have made this mistake.

The best thing to do when the plate is tipping over is to do the obvious—stop adding to it! Here is a hard truth: pride will keep you from admitting your need for help. Here is an even harder truth: the general mentality of many is that it is the ministry leader's responsibility to carry all of the weight. The easiest way to stop adding weight to your shoulders is to follow the sage advice of Jethro in the Bible. Jethro, Moses's father-in-law, was bringing Moses's wife and children back from their visit to his homeland. Moses, in his effort to meet the needs of the people, left his family with Jethro all day. Now, I don't know about you, but I can hear Jethro thinking, "Hold up! Wait a minute! I already raised my daughter. I gave her to you, and now you are giving her and your kids back to me! Not happening!" The Bible doesn't expressly say Jethro marched his daughter and grandchildren back to his son-in-law, but it does reveal Jethro's wisdom. Identifying responsible leaders and sharing responsibility alleviates burden. Jethro, as a family man and a leader, understood the principle of sharing the load (Exodus 18).

It's easy to become consumed with every affair that arises in the lives of those we lead. We have to remember two things: one, most problems brought to you can and should be solved by the ones who brought them to you; and two, when those problems can't be solved, trust that there are others who are equipped to do so. We point people to the One who "will supply every need" according to Philippians 4:19. In other words, we are guides—not saviors.

Training, equipping, and empowering others to share responsibility helps a leader remove some items from the plate.

5. Prioritize, delegate, and be intentional

Priority, delegation, and intentionality must become the guiding principles in creating the balance your family needs and deserves. The apostle Paul, in his first letter, admonishes Timothy twice about the importance of leading and providing for one's household. When we as ministry leaders don't set priorities, delegate often, and become intentional about creating space and time, a few things happen. We burn out trying to make all things happen for everyone without really helping anyone. Others do not grow and develop around us because there is no demand for them to. The greatest tragedy is that, while we're helping others for the sake of the ministry, our own families fade into the background and get only the residue and the stink of what's left over. Is it right? Nope. Does it happen? All the time! Does it need to stop? Absolutely!

Families need leadership first and often. Some of the greatest horror stories are born from the homes of leaders in ministry. This does not glorify God! In fact, it's a shame. The only way to combat the inequity of ministry plaguing our families is to honor them first and honor them often. Hear me, leader, when I say this: you have to get others involved early, involved throughout, and involved always. You will never make time for your family when your focus is always on the "ministry." Ministry is service, and service must begin at home first. Does this mean there won't be times when you'll have to tend to the needs of others you're responsible for leading? Absolutely not! However, you must not allow the constant bleating of sheep to drown out the cries of your family. Understand that too many leaders are stressed out and dying for ministries and people who couldn't care less, while the leader's family is left broken and drifting in the wake of destruction. It's time to get things in order! Make up your mind that family is a priority, then delegate things that get in the way of meeting that priority. Be intentional about creating balance. If you don't, something is always waiting to pounce and take away your most cherished gift—your family.

Her Eyes

Mom: My Greatest Joy and Sorrow

I grew up in an environment where my grandparents, both of my parents, and several family members served within the church in some capacity. They were ministers, deacons, mothers, Sunday School teachers, youth leaders, choir members, ushers, secretaries, and more. I was always in church. When I was growing up, church started with breakfast at 8:00 a.m. and ended with dinner around 3:00 p.m. This was every Sunday. If you think that was a lot, the church's two-week revival meetings had me at church from 8:00 a.m. to 10:00 p.m. on average! I am not exaggerating. That's just how it was. As a result of coming up in a family of people who served, I too began to serve in ministry. I started singing in the choir at age five, was a youth usher, and as I got older, served in leadership capacities within the youth and youth choir as well as working in our family-owned ice cream parlor within the church. In between all this "serving," I began getting involved in many of the things I saw as the "norm" within this particular church, including alcohol and sex. Sin was so rampant and accepted in this environment and I became a part of it all at a very young age. I even brought my boyfriend, who is now my husband, into this environment. At the age of sixteen, I was pregnant. Where I had become pretty good at covering up my involvement in this culture of sin, I was now exposed. I was the straight-A student, involved in school, community, and church, now very pregnant at sixteen.

Though it might seem that I would be devastated, I was overjoyed. Sure, my life was about to drastically change, but I didn't care. There was such a newfound joy and purpose that I had never experienced before. I had battled with depression and many suicide attempts as a preteen and teen, and this new life growing inside of me gave me hope and a reason to live. I gave birth in September of my senior year, finished high school on time, and enrolled in classes at the university for the summer. I was determined to continue pursuing my dreams and goals. My fiancé, now husband, enlisted in the United States Navy, we got married, and soon we were expecting our second child. My focus quickly shifted to raising my boys and ensuring they had everything they needed. My love and willingness to do anything for my children became my life. My husband was deployed a lot, and we now had four children, two boys and two girls, and therefore every dream I had for myself was put on hold. I still did some of the things I loved to do. I continued to sing, dance, and act in stage plays, but my focus and priority was my children. I attempted to return to college several times, but motherhood took precedence. I soon became wife, mom, and minister. At the time, I thought I was doing what was best for my family.

As a mother, I did the very best I could to remain involved in all of my children's activities. I was a den mother for Cub Scouts and Boy Scouts, a Girl Scout leader and cheerleading coach, a member of the booster club for the football team, and a board member for the PTSA. I attended most track meets and football games, and all award ceremonies and graduations. I also made sure my children maintained a 3.0 grade point average or above, they were prepared for college, and they were able to participate in most senior-year activities. My children were also involved in ministry. They sang in the choir, danced in the dance ministry, and were active in the children's, youth, and teen ministry. In other words, I did my very best to create as normal of a life as possible for my children even as the ministers', leaders', and pastors' kids. I thought everyone was good and well balanced.

It wasn't until they hit those pre-adult years that I realized the truth: my children felt everything I felt, saw everything I saw, and at this point in their lives had come to the conclusion they really didn't want anything to do with church or ministry. We didn't live hypocritical lives, nor were we ever involved in any drama or scandal. I asked, what did we do that caused you all to feel this way? I began to pray and ask God for forgiveness: "If I've lived a life before my children that caused them to turn from You, Lord please forgive me." It wasn't my life, but it was the mere fact that they were part of the expectations, the sacrifices, the separations, and the challenges. Because they were there with us, no matter how much we tried to shield them from certain aspects of ministry, my children were still deeply impacted by all the pain and suffering.

In April of 2015, our ministry hosted a family retreat. Initially we planned everything for a marriage retreat, but nothing seemed to be lining up. As a result, four families came out for team-building activities and fun that homed in on the importance of working together as a family unit and communicating within the family. These activities also exposed where the breakdowns were. While sitting around the bonfire, my daughter said something very profound. She said she was glad this had turned into a family retreat and not another marriage retreat because, while the husband and wife have one another to cope with life, who do the children really have? I thought, you have your other siblings and you always have mom and dad. What I did not realize was how lonely the call to ministry can be for the children of leaders, too.

Children's View: They Were There, Too

I have asked the oldest four of my six children to write a few sentences about how ministry affected them—the good, the bad, and the ugly, uncut and transparent. Here is what they said (these statements are not in order of birth and are anonymous).

Child 1: "Growing up as a PK (pastor's kid) was something I can't say I regret as it really became, for a while, all I knew. I love God with all my heart; however, I believe being a PK came with this expectation to immediately tap into our gifts, though we were always taught that we have to come at our own time and that there is partly an expectation just because of whose we were.

"I love my parents and love them as pastors, but growing up going to every event and living pretty much at church, I got tired of hearing about Jesus or God. I felt suffocated by it because I felt like, though God is everything, not every explanation in life has to go back to God. For a while I became rebellious, like most PKs, because of the built persona that life was okay because I went to church all the time. I knew who God was, but had no real relationship until I got a bit older and could understand it.

"Growing up in the church helped me grow as a man with wisdom, but I believe the hardest thing sometimes was to see Mom and Dad as Mom and Dad, not as the titles they had. At the end of the day, growing up in a church or raised in the streets, a kid just wants their mom and dad, and I feel like the family was put on the back burner for God's sake many times."

Child 2: "Ministry has affected me in many ways and has taught me so many things. Me personally, I've been affected by the good and the bad, lost some, gained some, and taken some big blows. Yet, at the end of the day, I still love it. It's one of the many things I see myself still doing in the future."

Child 3: "Growing up in ministry hasn't been all bad, honestly. The scriptures taught me how to endure, and that sacrifice was the cost of following Jesus. My biggest challenge was learning to be disciplined when my peers weren't, and there were times I wondered if I should have been 'bad' so that I could really 'feel' saved when I wasn't."

Child 4: "Growing up in ministry has taught me a lot, but has pushed me away from wanting to pursue it later in life. I've found it to be overbearing and at times unfair."

We also have two more children whom God has entrusted to us to raise as our own. While they are too young to input their view on ministry, we can honestly say that we have learned from our many mistakes. As we grow and know better, we all do better. It's very important to us to provide a balanced and healthy life for them.

LEADERSHIP NUGGET

Don't force your calling on your child/children. Save the pastoring for everyone else; to your children, be mom and dad.

After all that I've given to my children while trying to be a living example of Christ, I would have loved for each of these statements to be full of gratitude and appreciation, but I completely understand. Not to mention, we must give room for our children to come into a knowledge and true relationship with God, independent of Mom and Dad's prayer or calling. I listened to a very powerful interview with T.D. Jakes, and one statement that really stuck out to me was that your child can go anywhere in the world and find a pastor, but they only have one mother and father. Leaving a legacy is wonderful, and the desire that one day your children will take over the ministry or even walk alongside you in ministry is awesome. However, don't force your calling on your child. Walk with them and teach them, and be an example, a mentor, a disciplinarian, and a nurturer. Save the pastoring for everyone else, but, to your children, be Mom and Dad.

Unfortunately, I've seen too many leaders raise their children in ministry only to see them completely rebel against everything they were ever taught. It's so easy to blame ourselves for our children's experiences. It's so easy to feel shame. Leaders, it's not your fault and there is no reason to feel shame. Hurt and disappointment, sure, but not shame. Just as your life is full of testimony, of mistakes and victories, your children need room to experience the same. In a perfect world, we pray they are able to learn from our mistakes and not have a desire to repeat those same experiences. However, our hope can be found in the truth that, if we have trained up our children in the way they should go, when they are old they will not depart from it. They may detour for a bit, but we can continue to hope they will find love in Christ.

I'll tell you one thing: we haven't quite figured out how to balance it all, but what we do know is that we love and cherish our family very much. Making the small moments count has become priceless. We can never get time back and time waits for no one, so we embrace the time we have with our family. The responsibility and accountability of ministry don't make it easy, but it certainly is worth figuring out the balance for our families and for our sanity as Mom and Dad.

WHAT WE LEARNED: GOD'S EYES

Invest in creating memories. Take time off. Get away. Let your hair down and allow your children to let their hair down, too. Don't let the only memories you have be about ministry. Your family deserves to have something that is uniquely their own. When the only experiences you and your family have are related to ministry, those will be the only memories you have. Don't let that happen! Create memories exclusive to your family—build legacy!

Don't expect perfection from yourself or your children. It's tough enough that people will try to place you on a pedestal. Please don't let them place your children on that pedestal, too. Give them space to be children. They are going to make mistakes. It's inevitable. However, these are their mistakes and they are your children. Never let your ministry assignment blind you to your most important assignment in relation to them: parenting. Most importantly, make sure your children know they are your priority—not ministry, not work, not anything. Guard them!

Find your healthy balance. Family, ministry, work—there will always be something or someone vying for your time. More troubling is that each of these things is important. The key is to never neglect any one of them for too long. You won't notice it at first, but willfully ignoring any one of these creates stress and causes major breakdowns in the relationships that matter most. Failure to keep balance may cost you more than you're willing to pay.

Don't allow outside influences to upset your peace. I can't overstress the importance of guarding your peace and the peace of your family. It's often said that people don't care about you. That is not necessarily true. People care, but they care about themselves more. And they will upset your peace to get theirs. It's not personal. It is what it is. When you understand this, it makes saying yes to yourself and your family easier and empowering. Remember to prioritize your family and keeps you from feeling guilty for the most powerful word when others encroach on your peace: no!

REFLECTION
Questions for Discussion

1. What are your expectations of your children at home, school, community, and ministry?

2. Do you believe your expectations are reasonable and realistic?

3. When your children see your response to ministry, what do they see?

4. How do you ensure a healthy balance between your family and ministry?

5. What does quality time look like for you and your children?

6. Do you have planned periods of rest and vacations together?

7. Is it easier to be Mom or Dad to your children, or a pastor to many?

8. Reflect on one of the most memorable moments with your children. If you could share what made that moment so precious, what would it be? Why was it important? What did you learn from that moment?

Chapter 6

FAITH AND VISION
—FOCUSED PASSION

Up to this point, we have taken you on a journey into the hearts of two ministry leaders. We have endeavored to give you, although not comprehensive, a glimpse of our struggles, vulnerabilities, mistakes, and successes. Truthfully, it's safe to say we would have quit if it weren't for our faith in God and the vision He gave us.

Vision is the thing that keeps you going when everything else says, "Quit!" Why? Because you've already seen the end. You know what the outcome will be if you just keep going. It's the vision that got you going in the first place. If you're ready to throw in the towel, don't do it! Remember why you began and have faith that it will come to pass. You've got this!

LEADERSHIP NUGGET:

Success is really never about quantity—it's about endurance.

And I am convinced and sure of this very thing, that He Who began a good work in you will continue until the day of Jesus Christ [right up to the time of His return], developing [that good work] and perfecting and bringing it to full completion in you. —Philippians 1:6, AMPC

HIS EYES

Shortly after I gave my life to Christ (for real), I had a very disturbing dream. I saw myself standing on a massive stage, preparing to speak to a great gathering of people. The crowd was so large, it looked like a human sea. I was afraid, and yet I was at peace. I knew this was right where I was supposed to be. Prior to that point in the dream, I had been chased and shot at by gunmen, physically held down by people in ministry, and gagged in efforts to prevent me from speaking. All throughout the dream, I constantly found myself running and afraid. When I finally arrived at the platform, it didn't seem real. It felt like I was being thrust into a position of great responsibility without any clothes on. I truly believe God had given me a foreshadowing of my future life with Him, a vision.

Remaining true to the vision is easier said than done. It's hard. Not because the vision in and of itself is hard—it's the vision, and when it's from God, it doesn't change. It really is that simple. Staying true to it is hard because of the distractions and divisions that come with fulfilling the vision. There is always something pulling your attention out of focus. There is always something that comes to discourage you even when you've given your best. There is always a naysayer or someone who doesn't connect with the vision. That's okay. It's a part of the journey toward the vision. The key is to not allow any one of these to knock you off course. Let's consider each one of these hindrances in detail.

Distractions

Distractions can include anything from the busyness of life to major setbacks. Regardless of where it falls on the scale of severity, it is nonetheless a distraction. It's a distraction if it causes you to look in any other direction except toward the vision. Early in my adult walk with Christ (maybe three or four years in), a random stranger approached me in a clothing store and said something that sent chills down my spine. It absolutely terrified me. He called me a pastor. I immediately corrected him and told him I was just "everyday people." His reply, while gentle, was determined: "No, pastor. You are more than that."

I was still grappling with salvation issues and now here came someone out of the clear blue, telling me something I absolutely didn't want to hear. I thought, a pastor? Really? I see what pastors do, the amount of stress that comes with that job. No, thank you! I'm perfectly fine with sweeping, cleaning toilets, leading the youth, singing with the praise and worship team, picking up trash in the parking lots, helping administratively, and anything else the church needs. Besides, I don't have the training. I'm scared to death of speaking in front of people. I'm not qualified to be a pastor.

LEADERSHIP NUGGET

Don't be so distracted by your so-called shortcomings or inadequacies that you fail to see your qualifications.

Now, let me say this—no one can tell you who you are or what your assignment is. Only God has the authority to do that. The only thing people can do is agree with what the Father has already decreed concerning you. Deep in my heart, I knew I was called to walk in what some might refer to as the "ascension gifts" as defined in Ephesians 4. It was something spoken to me quietly by the Holy Spirit. I knew that what the man said was true, but I was distracted by fear, doubt, and insecurity.

These small seeds of distraction manifested quickly. Not long after this encounter, my family and I were stationed in Europe. In our search to locate and connect with a local assembly to worship and serve, I met up with an old fellow sailor and shipmate who was pastoring in one of the nearby towns. The irony is no one would have ever envisioned either one of us in ministry, let alone leadership. I hadn't seen him in nearly seven years—talk about a blast from the past! I wasn't prepared for what he said next. "My replacement has arrived!" Are you kidding me?! I thought God and I had settled this. I was not qualified. I was not educated enough.

I was not a pastor! Needless to say, I didn't go back. I ran. I ran to comfortable. I ran to easy. I ran right into complacency. Instead of trusting God in His omniscience, I chose to see my faults instead. The seeds of distraction ultimately cost me twelve years of purpose. I still stand by my former assessment that I wasn't ready; I wasn't. The problem wasn't my lack of readiness. It was that I didn't trust God to make me ready for the assignment. My distracted view wouldn't allow me to see it from His point of view and ultimately led to the long way around.

LEADERSHIP NUGGET

If you think you're ready, you aren't;
if you think you're not ready, you are.

Divisions

Fast-forward eleven years, and I was still not ready. And if we're all honest, there's never a time when we feel "ready" for the call of ministry (or anything of significance, for that matter). I had accepted the call, but I was serving two masters. I was still in the navy, but now God had given my wife and I a strong unction to plant a ministry (another step toward the vision) that could no longer be put off or ignored. The confirmation of that unction was affirmed at what I believed was the worst possible time in my naval career. I was headed back to an arduous assignment at sea. I remember thinking, are you kidding me? How am I supposed to do this now?

LEADERSHIP NUGGET

One of the greatest obstacles
to accomplishing vision is division.

I was divided. Let me unpack this a little. What do I mean when I say *divided?* I have found two major ways to be divided, and both of them can scuttle your success. You can be divided in your mind and in your time. When you are divided in your mind, every action you take, whether it's personal, professional, or relational, is affected. The Bible letter of James reminds us, "a double-minded man is unstable in all of his ways" (James 1:8, ESV). The divided mind creates instability, and that instability causes insecurity. Insecurity inevitably leads to erratic actions.

Fortunately, division of mind was not my dilemma. It was my time. My naval career and my ministry assignment were in conflict. My faith motivated me forward. Why? God had already given me His assurance. I didn't doubt the assignment, but I questioned the moment. My wife and I both knew this ministry assignment would be the last one before we launched the ministry we were called to birth. We knew God would lead us, but we didn't know when. It's easy to get lost in the "work" when you're in your season of next. In other words, when your motives are right, you go to work without worrying about your time in the spotlight. We were so busy supporting the vision of our leader that we gave little regard or preparation to the vision God had given us. So, when our time came, it seemed as if the timing was off.

LEADERSHIP NUGGET:

Focus on the work before you and not the dream ahead of you.

While I couldn't see it at the time, everything was aligning according to God's plan. God created an impossible situation (timing I couldn't control) so He would receive all of the glory (divine intervention). Shortly after we launched the ministry, I experienced a major health issue that ended my naval career. That career-ending issue happened four months after I completed my requirement for honorable military retirement and created time for my wife and me to give attention to the ministry. I could not have executed a timelier and more well-planned exit strategy. It was technically impossible. Yet, God did it. He made the time!

Leader-full Vision

There's an old adage that has been used in different variations by different people, but it simply says, "If it is to be, then it is up to me." I think this statement is only half true. Yes, you and I have a responsibility as leaders to have vision, but we must also connect those we lead to the vision. Achieving vision is about "us" and "we." Connecting "me" to the vision is easy; I'm closest to it. Connecting others . . . well, that's a totally differently matter altogether, especially when it comes to ministry.

LEADERSHIP NUGGET

Sometimes the connection between the vision and others is me.

If the vision were totally up to me to accomplish, then I would trust in my faith, gifts, talents, and abilities to get it done. The reality, however, is I am only one person; anything of significance is rarely accomplished without the help of others, and they need to be full of the vision, too. One of the earliest definitions of leadership I learned was this: the ability to get work done through others.

For years I had been responsible for leading and developing teams, but somehow that insight was lost in translation in the early stages of the ministry. I have personally come into contact with many a ministry leader who makes the same mistake—attempting to carry the load and the vision alone! I made the mistake with my wife, my children, and the ministry. How could I be successful in the military and private industry, and not in my private and ministry life? Easy—in the military and private industry, I was constantly reminded that no one is indispensable. Everyone can be replaced. Believe it or not, I enjoyed the security this provided. There is very little gray area. The rules are clear, and any violation of those rules is subject to disciplinary action. It keeps you focused on the mission. Even though everyone is essential in accomplishing the goal, there's always a sense that some might not make it. There will be some who won't be there when you get to the end. You focus on your part and on doing it well. Accomplish the mission.

There is often a "zero-defect" mentality when it comes to leadership. This is especially true when it pertains to home and/or ministry life. I say "especially" because of the deep levels of intimacy these environments entail. These parts of life are full of gray areas. I said earlier that there are rarely soft places to land in leadership. Now, for believers, the scriptures teach us that men are to be spiritual leaders in the home. Historically men have led in ministry, also. The responsibility is great and the expectations, whether implied or explicit, are weighty. They're felt, they're embodied, and they are too much. Men know it. And that's the rub. It's a rock-and-a-hard-place scenario playing out on a regular basis. Now, I know you might say, "Well, that's just your perception." You're probably right, but let's have that conversation after you fail a family member, or after something falls through the cracks in ministry when you couldn't be everything to everyone when they needed you most.

Family and ministry demand a near-perfect performance. In the places where grace should abound, there is rarely room for failure. This is why it's important to share the vision and connect people to it. As others become more vested, they become more responsible, and with responsibility comes accountability. When you are the only one with the vision, you bear the responsibility of carrying it out. As sure as you are reading this, they will hold you accountable.

Her Eyes

A great leader's courage to fulfill his vision comes
from passion, not position. —John Maxwell

From the birth of our ministry, we knew there would be challenges because God gave us a ministry based on kingdom principles with a mission to develop kingdom ambassadors for a global impact. We were given the mandate to train, equip, empower, and release or send leaders to fulfill their purpose. The vision of the ministry was huge, a vision we knew there was no way we could ever complete on our own. We had to walk completely and totally in faith. For six years, everything seemed to be going well. We went from having service in our home to, with the help of some amazing people, owning property and land. We went from having a home daycare and homeschooling to having our own private Christian school.

My faith was strong and my passion was my drive. With everything in me, I knew what God said, and I knew the vision He gave us as a couple, me as His daughter, and the ministry as a whole. I was determined and persistent about doing everything I could in my own strength to ensure the vision came to pass. I was determined to do my part and do it well. There was a great passion and fire within me that would not allow me to quit or deviate from the vision. Let me walk you through some of the things you'll need to do to see your God-given vision fulfilled.

> Where there is no vision, the people perish: but he that keepeth the law, happy is he. — Proverbs 29:18, KJV

1. Remain true to the vision and trust the process

I believe when God gives you a vision, that vision does not change. The assignments along the way will change, the directions in which we go to fulfill that vision may change, but the goal of the end product remains the same. Once you understand your purpose as a leader, or your "why," your passion becomes your drive to fulfill the God-given vision. Hold on to the vision and trust the process. Faith, trust, and obedience became my everything, and you better believe they were tested and in most instances, proved. In the seventh year of ministry, when the ministry and school appeared to be a little shaky, those closest to me walked away, became the naysayers and backbiters. With each negative phone call and each unnecessary and unwanted conversation, my passion became stronger and stronger. I was not going to give up. I made sure my finish was just as strong as my start. I was determined!

I couldn't be concerned about what people thought. My focus wasn't even on who was with me and who wasn't. I believed with everything in me that whoever needed to be on my team for this leg of the race would be sent by God. I welcomed the persecution, the breaking, the crushing, because I knew that anything I had was nothing compared to what God had for me. There was no way I could lose with God. There is no way you will lose with God. Follow His plan and you will win every single time. I looked forward to the unknown and the new beginning. The fact that God thought enough of me to give me another opportunity to get it right causes me to be even more humble and grateful.

2. Beware when everyone speaks well of you

To be fair, this is what can be seen with the natural eye. As stated earlier, we were financially strapped. Our building, land, and home were about to go into foreclosure. We let go of the building. We finished out the school year, then had to begin the search for a new location. Our credit was shot, there was no real income, and the people were losing hope, almost begging us to walk away. Not to walk away from ministry, but to walk away from the institution, what the church had become. Anger, frustration, regret, bitterness, and selfishness began to settle. They weren't creeping in—they were already here and beginning to settle. Nevertheless, there was still a vision from God, an even greater faith, and a passion that burned deep within me, and no matter what, I was not going to smite the rock. I was not going to detour from the vision and plan of God. My yes was still my yes and my obedience to God would always outweigh the desires of men, including my own.

I shared with you earlier that we had to do a reset. We had to reevaluate and regain our passion in order to move forward in faith and continue toward fulfilling the vision. Once we made the decision to take the sabbatical, I was fueled with invigoration and creativity. My passion was still alive and I wanted to keep going, but in another direction. The vision didn't change, but the method did. However, as a result of our decision and move in another direction of ministry, the whispers, assumptions, and accusations began to spread across the community. Not once did anyone pick up the phone and ask a single question. Not once, yet entire stories were put together based on false assumptions. Prior to this, those same people were praising us and supporting us for the positive impact we were having within the community. There was praise coming from everywhere, but the moment we decided to shut it all down, reset, and go back to the original plan, there was a different response.

In Luke 6:26 (MSG), Jesus tells the disciples, "There's trouble ahead when you live only for the approval of others, saying what flatters them, doing what indulges them. Popularity contests are not truth contests—look how many scoundrel preachers were approved by your ancestors! Your task is to be true, not popular." If everyone is always in agreement with you, praising your every move, you have to ask yourself, am I pleasing people or God?

Leaders, there is no cookie-cutter way to flow in your ministry. As I write this chapter, the world is experiencing a pandemic due to the COVID-19 virus (coronavirus). The world is in a state of quarantine and temporarily forced to adapt to a lifestyle of staying at home and social distancing. The churches are closed and ministry leaders are challenged to think outside the four walls of the church and really be the church. I believe God is resetting everything and everybody. He is readjusting and realigning our focus to be put back on Him as Christ builds His church—talk about an uprooting, destroying, tearing down, and rebuilding. Leaders have created idols and empires within the church and used the sanctuary to build them. God has removed all of that and forced the church and the leaders to be still and know that He is God. I believe the call and mandate to go back to the beginning has become the prevalent and pertinent message for all believers.

In the beginning, God created us with a purpose and plan. We have deviated from the original plan and purpose for our lives and allowed the influence of everything else to trump everything God said, and now we have a choice. We can continue to try to do things our way for popularity and numbers, or go back to the original plan of advancing God's agenda, the original vision. Keeping the vision before you to help keep you focused and centered is something every leader should practice. Again, how you get there, the methods you use, your resources, your team and location, may all change, but I believe the final destination will not change. Stay true to the process and remain focused, full of passion, in order to stay on course for the vision.

WHAT WE LEARNED
GOD'S EYES

Where there is no vision [no redemptive revelation of God], the people perish; but he who keeps the law [of God, which includes that of man]—blessed (happy, fortunate, and enviable) is he. —Proverbs 29:18, AMPC

There is no vision if God is not in it. Thinking on the history of the great cruise liner, the RMS *Titanic*, an unknown crewmember is remembered to have said, "God himself could not sink this ship!" What a bold statement! It's one thing to be confident, but it's a totally different animal altogether when humankind believes its greatest achievements are incapable of being subject to the will and hand of the One who created us all. There is often a lot of "I" and "me" language associated with how people describe vision. And while it's important to take responsibility for the vision, we must remember Who gave us the vision to begin with. Following any vision that excludes God is like setting a baby loose in the wilderness and expecting him/her to survive—it just doesn't make sense!

Agree with the vision and then commit. Vision is like dancing with a partner: it feels awkward until you are in agreement with your partner completely and you are fully committed to the outcome—a beautifully envisioned, choreographed, and performed piece for all to enjoy. Tamara is a dancer. Lawrence can dance. Here is the difference: one of us totally embodies the art of dance with action, while the other enjoys the beauty of it through observance. Individually, it becomes clear which one is lacking, but if the one who lacks chooses to agree and commit to the one who has more, then the one who is lacking becomes better. It is essential for the one with less knowledge, less skill, and less ability to acknowledge and agree (trust) that the one with more not only has more to offer, but sees more, too. The wills must merge so that the two may become one. The one with less (you) has to come up (commit) to where the greater one (God) is in order for the piece (vision) to flow. Put plainly, unity is powerful, and when we agree with God and His vision, it brings unparalleled success personally and for the community at large.

Let faith be your passion. Giving up all for the vision is admirable, but that's not all there is to it. You have to have a fire that rages deep within, pushing, pulling, and if need be, dragging you into the manifestation of the vision. That's passion! It's not blind passion, stumbling and fumbling around in the dark. Instead, it is faith-filled, focused, purposed, and determined to hit the bull's-eye! You need passion when the vision isn't as clear as when you started. Faith is vision, and vision is what God has said about your future. It is the essence of the thing hoped for. It is the thing seen long before it ever materializes.

This is what the writer of Hebrews 11 refers to when he says, "Now faith is the substance of things hoped for, the evidence of things not seen" (NKJV). But "hope" and "things not seen" often appear to be mystical creatures when you are facing what look like insurmountable odds. Adversity, failure, pain, and discouragement all come when you are pursuing what isn't yet. The notable key is "yet." Knowing there is a "yet" in front of you is the fuel propelling you closer to the "now" of your vision. There will be times when the vision seems far off. That's okay. Everyone won't see your vision. That's all right, too. There may be times when you have difficulty believing in yourself or moments when others don't believe in you, but under no circumstances should you ever lose your fire, the God-given passion that keeps you driving toward the prize.

REFLECTION
Questions for Discussion

1. What is the vision you believe God gave you when you first started your leadership journey?

2. Do you feel you have remained true to the vision, or deviated from the original plan?

3. List a few of your accomplishments toward the vision.

4. How do you overcome the challenge of distractions?

5. In what areas of the vision has your faith been tested?

6. Does your team clearly know your vision, mission, and purpose?

7. Describe in one sentence what you are most passionate about.

8. If no one bought into your vision, would you have the passion to keep going?

Chapter 7

LEADERS WHO WIN

Throughout this journey, we have dropped small nuggets along the way to lead you to this point. If you haven't figured it out by now, leaders who win are persistently pursuing, pushing, pressing, persevering, and progressing toward and into promise. To quote a common cliché, "It's not easy, but it's worth it." This is the testimony of every leader who wins! No leader wins, however, without bringing it all together. Here's what we hope you've learned so far. Leaders who win:

- answer the call

- sacrifice, sacrifice, sacrifice

- build strong partnerships

- create and protect balance

- see the vision and keep on seeing it until it's done (and then they see the next thing)

So, why must leaders win?

> My whole life, meeting people is like a blind date, because I feel like they've already seen the video on me. —Michael J. Fox

The life of the servant leader is always on display. People see the video, make assumptions, come to conclusions, and execute judgments without ever taking time to do life with the leader.

The minister's life is polished—not because he/she chooses for it to be, but because it's what the video demands. No one buys the production process. No one cares about what happens behind the scenes. People want the thing that's "shiny," and they want it now. But, like a shiny new toy, the luster of ministry's appeal often fades and soon becomes nothing more than a dull, nagging ache.

In spite of the pain, the minister marches onward like a good soldier—head high, ignoring the pain—knowing danger is ahead, but convinced the sacrifice is for the greater good. This becomes exponentially more challenging when other factors are involved in ministry's call (i.e., spouse, children, employment, etc.). There is a dynamic at play. It can be likened to the flying trapeze act in a circus. For five minutes, the crowd "oohs" and "ahhs" at each death-defying stunt, but no one really comprehends the strength, synchronicity, and sacrifice invested by each artist personally and combined. Here is the rub: if the act fails, if someone gets hurt, if the trapeze artist dies, the crowd will go to the show the following year. They will expect the same awe-inspiring acts with little regard for the impact of the loss suffered. The show must go on.

LEADERSHIP NUGGET

Don't do what you do because others are watching;
do it because God is watching!

OUR EYES: HOW LEADERS WIN

1. Invest in yourself and in your team

This may shake your theology: Jesus was selfish. Before you pick up stones, let us explain. He needed to be selfish to be selfless. Despite the assignment on His life to "be about His Father's business," His humanity required time alone in prayer (spiritual); development of understanding (mental; He masterfully used the Scriptures to defeat the Adversary); and sleep, food, and drink (physical).

We cannot say this enough: you can't give what you don't have. We'll say that again: you can't give what you don't have. As a leader, whether it's at home, on the job, or in the community, the demand is constant. There will always be someone or something that requires attention. That's not a bad thing. It's just the way it is. When you don't take time to invest in yourself (spiritually, mentally, and physically), there will be a breakdown.

LEADERSHIP NUGGET

Your purpose on this planet requires your best
—not your leftovers.

When was the last time you actually did something that significantly contributed to your well-being? Do you remember? When was the last time you read for enjoyment, went on a real vacation, or just enjoyed God's creation? When was the last time you exercised? Do you find yourself seated behind the steering wheel of your car, cramming a meal down your throat en route to the next meeting or event? Have you taken that self-improvement class yet? What does your house look like? While the questions may make you uncomfortable, they are necessary in order to determine the degree to which you are investing in yourself and the quality of what you are pouring out to those with whom you have influence. It almost goes without saying: if you're toxic or empty, then what others receive from you will be, too.

The same is true for your team. Encourage them to invest in themselves. Investing in your personal wellness and development helps you grow as a leader. The same kind of investment is paramount for your team. When you don't encourage those you lead to practice self-care, burnout will happen, their leadership capacity will plateau, and the results will multiply negatively throughout your organization. You should always seek ways to help your team grow. Don't fear their growth. It makes everyone better. Invest in them and they will pour back into the vision greatly.

2. Set and maintain boundaries

When you have a heart for people and a deep desire to see them operate at their greatest potential, it's difficult to not become deeply invested in them. In fact, you will do life together. While the rewards are quite fulfilling, it can be a detriment to your well-being, also. As much as we would love to tell you that every relationship you encounter in ministry is all roses and bubbles, that simply is not reality. It may be for this reason, and this reason alone, that you must set boundaries. Does this mean you isolate yourself from people? Of course not! However, if you're the leader, everyone will not have the same responsibility or the same accountability that you have. This means everyone can't have the same access to you.

One of our apostles shared some wisdom with us that we will never forget: know those who are sent to you, and those who are sent for you. Those who are sent *to* you are the individuals you have the anointing to empower, train, and equip for the next leg of their journey. They are sent to you so you can pour into them. Those who are sent *for* you are individuals that have the anointing, time, talent, and treasure you need to transition into the next leg of the journey. They connect with the vision, assist you with the execution, and allow you to see and shift into the next stage of God's plan for you. Know the difference and set some boundaries. Unfortunately, while people say they want you to be transparent, you will find that sometimes your transparency with the wrong people does more damage than good. Everyone can't be in your inner circle. Discern who is sent to you and who is sent for you, and set your boundaries.

3. Empower your team

Because you were never meant to do anything alone, empower your team so together everyone wins. Honor and allow every gift from your team to be fully utilized. There is no room for pride or for possessive obsession. In simple terms, don't micromanage! Teach and train each member to effectively activate and implement their gifts. Get everyone actively involved in everything. Each gift has purpose and adds value to the overall vision. Don't be intimidated or consider your gifts any greater than the gifts within your team. For a great example of the importance of team empowerment, remember the wisdom Jethro imparts to Moses regarding leadership:

> And so it was, on the next day, that Moses sat to judge the people; and the people stood before Moses from morning until evening. So when Moses' father-in-law saw all that he did for the people, he said, "What is this thing that you are doing for the people? Why do you alone sit, and all the people stand before you from morning until evening?" And Moses said to his father-in-law, "Because the people come to me to inquire of God. When they have a difficulty, they come to me, and I judge between one and another; and I make known the statutes of God and His laws." So Moses' father-in-law said to him, ***"The thing that you do is not good. Both you and these people who are with you will surely wear yourselves out. For this thing is too much for you; you are not able to perform it by yourself."***—Exodus 18:13–18, NKJV

Another example is in Ephesians. Just before Jesus ascended into heaven, he gave some gifts—apostles, prophets, evangelists, pastors, and teachers—

> . . . to fully equip and perfect the saints (God's people) for works of service, to build up the body of Christ [the church]; until we all reach oneness in the faith and in the knowledge of the Son of God, [growing spiritually] to become a mature believer, reaching to the measure of the fullness of Christ [manifesting His spiritual completeness and exercising our spiritual gifts in unity]. From Him the whole body [the church, in all its various parts], joined and knitted firmly together by what every

joint supplies, when each part is working properly,
causes the body to grow and mature, building itself
up]in [unselfish] love. —Ephesians 4:12–16, AMP

A dormant gift is untapped potential. Don't be the cause of your team not operating in the fullest potential. Empower everyone and win together!

LEADERSHIP NUGGET:

*You can't effectively lead while trying to do everything yourself,
so empower your team to lead with you.*

---

4. Set realistic expectations for yourself and your team

Leadership takes effort, and building a solid team can be even more challenging. Setting realistic expectations that are attainable is extremely important. We all have standards that we set for ourselves and we have those same expectations for our team to uphold those standards. This is a good and necessary principle. Every successful organization has high standards for its leadership, its team, and the services it offers. Strive for excellence in everything you do. As leaders, you absolutely should! However, we can set unrealistic expectations for both ourselves and our team that will only bring frustration and disappointment. These are some realistic expectations to set for yourself:

Build your faith. Pray, read, meditate, study, teach, lead, listen, obey, and testify.

Remain healthy. In all areas of your life—physical, mental, spiritual, and financial—leave nothing in an unhealthy state or out of balance.

Give your all. Live a life that is completely sold out and poured out before the Father.

Walk in integrity and wholeness. Don't leave room for anyone to question your character.

When you, as the leader, build your faith through studying, praying, fasting, and consecrating yourself, you will remain healthy. When you are healthy, you are then in a position to give your team your best. At the end of it all, not only in the presence of other people, but in the presence and eyes of God, you want to be men and women of integrity. You don't want to give anyone fuel to tear you and your character down. These expectations are realistic and attainable. They say victory and scream that this is a leader who wins.

Now, let's consider some realistic expectations for your team:

Build your faith. Encourage your team to pray, read, meditate, study, teach, lead, listen, obey, and testify. Require no more from your team than God requires of you.

Empower someone else and continue to grow. Encourage your team to invest their time, talent, and treasure into someone else. Where there is no growth, there is no fruit.

Give your all. Everyone has a very important role on the team. Whatever your role, no matter how big or small it may seem, give it one hundred percent.

Have integrity and be accountable. Accountability establishes ownership within the team. Your integrity protects your character. As a leader, not holding your team accountable will ultimately leave you carrying all of the weight (and they will let you, too). Don't be afraid to hold them accountable.

Remain healthy. Encourage your team to take care of themselves mentally, physically, spiritually, and financially.

5. Be willing to shift as God commands

Leaders, you can't get comfortable and become complacent. In Genesis 12, God told Abraham to leave everything behind, his country, his family, and everyone close to him, to go to a place that God would show him. He didn't know where God was going to lead him, but Abraham obeyed and moved. You must be willing and open to change, willing to shift and move as the Holy Spirit moves. Learn to receive and recognize when God is trying to do a new thing. Embrace change whether you like it or not. Who ever said any of this would be easy or comfortable? Thank God for the shifts and stretching in your life. Allow Him to take you into the unfamiliar in order to bring you into the greater thing that He has promised you. Don't get stuck!

6. Respond with wisdom and avoid reacting with emotions

One of the biggest mistakes is reacting with emotions instead of responding with wisdom. Ask God for wisdom and He will give it to you.

> If you need wisdom, ask our generous God, and He will give it to you. He will not rebuke you for asking. — James 1:5, NLT

Apply that wisdom to every situation. Don't make hasty decisions. Even when you're pressured to give a response, take a moment and respond with wisdom. What is wisdom? It's the quality of knowing how to use experience, knowledge, and good judgment. Use wisdom to discern who is for you and who is against you. Use wisdom in correction and in guidance. Apply wisdom to finances and resources. Apply wisdom when choosing whom you allow into your innermost circle. Apply wisdom to everything! Don't move without it.

7. Focus on the bigger picture

There will always be that little thing that can potentially become a big thing if you allow it to. Keep the main thing the main thing, and you'll not only win, but also gain a spirit of unity and unified purpose among your team. When the entire team is focused on the bigger picture, the potential arising of the occasional "I" tantrum is minimal, if at all. Don't ignore or become insensitive to the personal issues and challenges your team is facing. Confront the issue, challenge, or problem, then agree on the best way ahead. Ensure the team members' needs are met and everyone can move forward in a healthy way. You can't allow everyone's issues and emotions to become your personal issues and emotions; otherwise, you'll slow the entire team down. Learn to resolve issues quickly, delegate when possible, redirect attention, and turn the focus back to an overall purposed destination. Be sensitive and show that you care, but stay focused on the main thing.

REFLECTION
Questions for Discussion

1. What steps have you taken to invest in yourself?

2. What steps have you taken to invest in your team?

3. Why do you feel it's important to set boundaries?

4. What unrealistic expectations have you set for yourself and/or your team? Why?

5. What is the best advice you would give another leader about responding with wisdom?

6. What are the top three ways you empower your team?

7. What do you do to help yourself and your team remain focused on the bigger picture?

8. In what areas of leadership do you see a need for improvement, and what will be your strategy to implement any changes that are necessary?

CONCLUSION

Hello again, Friend—you made it! You've reached the beginning. We say "beginning" because this is where the work really begins. Hopefully you've had the opportunity to reflect along this journey. Winning involves a great deal of reflection, personal sacrifice, and intentionality.

Yet, with all of that, more is still required. It's the one thing we reserved until this chapter, but that should have subtly stood out throughout the book. What is it? It's steady and persistent application!

> It is not that I have already obtained it or already reached the goal—no, I keep pursuing it in the hope of taking hold of that for which the Messiah Yeshua took hold of me. Brothers, I, for my part, do not think of myself as having yet gotten hold of it; but one thing I do: forgetting what is behind me and straining forward toward what lies ahead, I keep pursuing the goal in order to win the prize offered by God's upward calling in the Messiah Yeshua. —Philippians 3:12–14, CJB

There are many obstacles along the path to reaching the vision God has given you. Sadly, too many quit just before reaching the goal. The reasons are legitimate—discouragement, discontentment, bitterness, anger, and financial distress, just to name a few. Know that what you are feeling is designed to refine you; these obstacles are tests of your resolve. This is not to say that they don't hurt. We know they hurt, but remember, "all things work together for good to them that love God, to them who are the called according to his purpose" (Romans 8:28, KJV). Life in ministry beyond the pulpit is not pretty. We apologize on behalf of every leader who has ever glamorized leadership. After the sermon is over and everyone has left the building, you still have to live, be, and function outside of church. After you have ministered to everyone else, you still have to minister to yourself, your spouse, and your children.

In conclusion, every leader must go through a process of proving, testing, and suffering. Most leaders can and will come out victorious, better equipped, and prepared for the next go-round. Just remember, hold fast in knowing that, in the beginning, you were part of an amazing plan. We have shared transparent views of a life beyond the pulpit from a husband and wife team in ministry. However, it is our prayer that you will read the last line of this book and know that God's view is really the final view. Go through the process and apply God's principles of leadership. If you do, you and your team will be better equipped for life beyond the pulpit and become leaders who win!

REFLECTION
Questions for Discussion

1. How has this book been a blessing to you?

2. Which principles, points, or leadership nuggets were most impactful?

3. How has this book affected your view of your leadership beyond the pulpit?

Made in the USA
Middletown, DE
09 October 2020

21485184R00057